Eternal Moment

Sándor Weöres

Eternal Moment

Selected Poems

Edited, and with an introduction, by Miklós Vajda

Foreword by William Jay Smith

Afterword by Edwin Morgan

Drawings by Sándor Weöres

Translated from the Hungarian by
Alan Dixon
Daniel Hoffman
Hugh Maxton
Edwin Morgan
William Jay Smith
George Szirtes

NEW RIVERS PRESS

Introduction translated by J. E. Sollosy

In association with Corvina Press, Budapest
and Anvil Press Poetry, London

ISBN 0-89823-101-9

CONTENTS

FOREWORD

LONG RECOGNIZED as a major poet in a country of many talented poets, Sándor Weöres was born in 1913 in Szombathely in western Hungary and was brought up in the neighboring village of Csönge. He was the son of a noble family; one of his ancestors became rich by selling supplies to the Napoleonic armies. Family tradition has it that there was a Gypsy chieftain among his ancestors, and the existence of such a figure may account for Weöres's dark, smoky eyes and for his lifelong interest in ancient Oriental culture and traditions. His father was a landowner and an officer in the Austro–Hungarian army. Weöres grew up speaking both German and Hungarian; at the age of nine or ten his German governess read Goethe, Schiller, and Heine to him. He attended the University of Pécs, first as a law student, then as a student of geography and history. He eventually took a doctorate in philosophy and aesthetics. In his doctoral dissertation, published in 1939 under the title *The Birth of the Poem*, he set forth his own principles of composition.

Weöres was something of a child prodigy, composing poetry even as an infant. "The prattle which started in the cradle," he has said, "was gradually transformed into conscious versification at the age of four or five." At the age of fifteen he wrote these lines:

> I am now at the end of my career;
> You, youngster, follow in my footsteps.

His career was then just beginning, but throughout his life the publication of each new volume has marked a new beginning, and he has never at any time lost the spirit of youth.

During the forties Weöres worked as a librarian and a museum administrator in various cities. In 1945 he retired to his native village of Csönge and became for a time a farmer. When he was nineteen, several of his poems were accepted for publication in the leading magazine *Nyugat* (West) by its editor, the well-known poet Mihály Babits. In 1935 and again in 1936 he received the Baumgarten Prize, considered at the time the highest literary award in Hungary. During World War II he was drafted into the labor force, but was never sent to the front. Since 1951 he has lived in Budapest and has devoted himself solely to his writing.

Weöres has traveled widely in Europe and has been to Egypt, Turkey, and the Soviet Union. His two visits to the Far East have had a great impact upon his work. He went to Manila in 1937 to take part in an Eucharistic Congress, and continued on to India and Vietnam. In 1948–49 he spent a year in Italy, and in 1959 visited China. As a translator of the Ukrainian poet Shevchenko, he was invited to Kiev in 1964, and as a translator of Rustaveli, he attended the celebration in honor of the Georgian poet in Tbilisi in 1966. In most of his travels since 1947 he has been accompanied by his wife, Amy Károlyi, a poet in her own right and a translator of Emily Dickinson. As guests of the Translation Center of Columbia University, Sándor Weöres and Amy Károlyi visited the United States in 1977 at the time of the publication of *Modern Hungarian Poetry*, edited by Miklós Vajda, by Columbia University Press. Together with Ferenc Juhász and István Vas, they read their poems to large audiences at the Guggenheim Museum in New York and at the Library of Congress in Washington, and they travelled to New England and to the West Coast.

Today acknowledged as one of the most important poets in the history of Hungarian literature, Sándor Weöres is unequalled in his mastery of the language. His work in a great variety of forms has brought him world renown and the admiration and friendship of poets in many countries. The wide range of his work makes it difficult to compare him with any other modern poet. For the depth of his lyricism, he calls to mind Rainer Maria Rilke or Dylan Thomas; in his philosophical and religious intensity he suggests T. S. Eliot or Paul Valéry; in his playful handling of language he evokes Christian Morgenstern.

To find a poet of similar range and virtuosity, one who can write inspired rhymes for children and who, as a visionary, can speak in near-prophetic measures of man's place in the universe one must turn to William Blake. Sándor Weöres is right in claiming that he finds the same mentality and the same sense of mission in Blake's works as in his own.

Weöres's subject is nothing less than man's place not just in the world but in the cosmos. His entire work is an effort to make a whole of the fragmentation of man's experience past and present. In examining the myths of other countries and other civilizations, he weaves his own myth around his own existence. He acknowledges a wide range of influences all the way from ancient Chinese poetry, Lao Tse, the Upanishads, the Bhagavad Gita, the Babylonian epic of Gilgamesh and the Egyptian hymns all the way to Negro mythology and the Polynesian Rabie Hainuvele cycle of myths. In an interview Weöres once said that he saw himself as a little man with a big head who happens to be passing through a room. There is nothing at all remarkable about this little man, he said: he is simply the medium through which the universe expresses itself.

The poet is one who in the words of Weöres must "retain the childhood, embryonic or perhaps even pre-conception quintessence of our being." The poet gives expression to the archetypal patterns of man's collective unconscious (and in this Weöres comes close to a Jungian view of the human psyche), unimpeded and open to change and experiment. "I think," he has said, "one should explore everything. Including those things which will never be accepted, not even in the distant future. We can never know, at the start of an experiment, where it will lead. Perhaps it will be an abortive, still-born enterprise, perhaps it will be a necessary and useful experiment—only we cannot know that, not even after we have completed it. It may take decades or centuries to prove whether it was a useful experiment or a useless one. It may never be proved at all. . . . The possibility that this poem or that one led nowhere does not worry me in the least. I never think about it."

Such an openness and willingness to experiment lends a constant freshness to everything that Weöres touches. He seems never to lose a childlike sense of wonder. He invents incessantly—new characters, new rhythms, even in some cases new languages. No modern poet, not even W. H. Auden, has written in such a variety of forms and shown himself master of them all. He ranges from simple nursery rhymes to sophisticated epigrams. He has a strong visual imagination and has produced witty line drawings and imaginative concrete poems. He can be incisive and profoundly moving; he can also be obscene, vulgar, and at times very funny. He has written long philosophical and satirical poems as well as explicitly erotic ones.

Critics have sometimes complained that Weöres is too esoteric and detached, but although he was never a political poet, his poems have sometimes dealt directly with the political and social scene. In 1953 he wrote a poem "Le Journal" which speaks of the fifties exactly as they were in Hungary and yet reads as if transformed by myth. However abstract Weöres becomes, he is always sensuous in his language. His great poems resemble the works of Mozart: they have a surface sweetness and delicacy that covers over a deep underlying tragedy.

"In such a poet," Edwin Morgan, the British translator of Weöres, has written, "it is natural that there should go with all this a deep sense of the interconnections of human and non-human life. These connections, felt more strongly by Weöres than the everyday props and ligatures of social institutions and habits, have sometimes given him a reputation for withdrawnness or pessimism that this work as a whole does not in fact show. Yet although he is obviously not writing for a mass audience, his poetry is so sinewy with energy, so ready to break out into wonder or playfulness that its 'black' qualities must be placed in that broader context of abounding creative pleasure. Even the bitter 'Internus', with its unrelieved catalogue of human failings, its Baudelairean nest of disgusts, has its positives; they emerge in the cleansing, purging power of an artist's 'No!,' something utterly distinct from the cynically negative positions the consciously reflective social mind might throw up:

> The panic world is baffled at my gate:
> 'Madman! Egotist! Traitor!' its words beat.
> But wait: I have a bakehouse in my head,
> you'll feed someday on this still uncooled bread.

At the end of 'Internus' the poet imagines his death as a return to the great plenum from which everything is continuously poured."

It is a paradox that the baker in this case is at the same time a conscious artist and a kind of mage. In a recent poem Weöres sees genius as a candle lit in a distant window at night, hardly bright enough to illuminate the interior of the room but a guiding signal to the wanderer:

Its flicker marks
the direction of my village
like a huge bonfire
across the night.

Weöres believes that the poet's mission is to speak for the whole man; he is one "who, if born with the gift of poetry, will use this gift well." Using his gift means for Weöres writing poetry that will move his readers so that they cannot remain indifferent, even if they do not understand it fully. This sense of Blakean mission he expressed as a very young man in his doctoral dissertation *The Birth of the Poem* and later defined explicitly in the introduction to *Springs of Fire* (1964): "My goal is not to provoke enthusiasm or irritation, nor to wish to be simply unusual. I want something different; I want to send out a ray of light that will shake the entire being, instinct, feelings, comprehension, imagination and spirit. The reader reads the poem but the poem also reads the reader. I want to radiate through the reader and shake him so that he will give up his closed, final, existential singular 'I' for the benefit of the open, social, cosmic, and endless plural 'I's.'"

The metaphor of flame occurs often in the recent poems of Weöres, as in "Song: Boundless Space":

When I was no one yet,
light, clear light,
in the winding brooks
I often slept.

As I almost became someone
a great force rolled me,
stone, rough stone,
ice-veined, down the slope.

And, finally, I have brightened
to live, flame, naked flame,
in rounded, boundless space,
showing our real country.

In one of his most striking long poems, "The Lost Parasol", two lovers lie down in the grass on the edge of a wild gorge, and when they arise, the girl leaves behind her red parasol. The poem describes in magnificent detail the slow disintegration of the forgotten parasol, with its flashing red silk and bone handle, in the driving wind and rain. As nature changes, the lovers also change, and the parasol is slowly transformed; invaded by vines, by worms and lizards, it settles in the brambles and goes slowly to pieces until only a tuft of red silk floats off into space. The lovers are lost in nature like the parasol, which, literally with its bone handle and its red silk, physically symbolizes their love. The merging of the parasol with space calls to mind a delicate Chinese print, and ndeed this poem unfolds in its wealth of detail like a misty Chinese scroll. The object of civilization is destroyed by nature, which continues to reproduce itself: the two lovers become one only in the song of the poet, which is eternal. Nowhere has Weöres more beautifully expressed his vision of the artist's triumph than in the concluding stanza:

> The red silk parasol was my song,
>   sung for my only one;
> this true love is the clearest spring,
>   I have smoothed its mirror with my breath,
> I have seen the two of us, the secret is known:
>   we shall moulder into one after death.
> Now I expend my life exultantly
> like the oriole in the tree:
> till it falls down on the old forest floor,
> singing with such full throat its heart must burst and soar.

WILLIAM JAY SMITH

INTRODUCTION

THE SEVENTY poems included in this volume are a modest introduction to a prolific life's work further screened by an accidental factor, that of translatability. It is not the poet's first appearance in English: in 1970 twenty-four Weöres poems were published in Edwin Morgan's translation in a volume of poems by Weöres and Ferenc Juhász, in the Penguin Modern European Poets series. However, this book was not given the reception it deserved; besides, it has long since been out of print. Weöres's writings have appeared in several other European languages as well. His name is familiar to those with a special interest in verse, but his presence is nevertheless marginal and in no way proportionate to his achievement.

In Hungarian, the Weöres œuvre includes three weighty volumes (over one thousand eight hundred pages) of poetry, and another three (almost two thousand five hundred pages) of poetry translations. His verse plays and plays for children make up another volume (of nearly five hundred pages). Furthermore, the unusual two-volume (almost one thousand pages long) anthology of forgotten or previously undiscovered gems of Hungarian poetry entitled *Három veréb hat szemmel* ('Three Sparrows with Six Eyes'), compiled, annotated and introduced by Weöres, is also regarded as part of his work. His own articles, prose works, interviews, comments on his experiments, as well as letters documenting the birth of some of his work, have been published here and there but not systematically. His œuvre is the subject of several books* and countless in-depth studies, and after long years of official neglect, it seems that he has taken his rightful place in Hungarian literature at last, though there is no consensus amongst his critics. His popularity with readers is unparalleled, though this is true only of certain parts of his work. The poet himself is still with us; he will be seventy-five in 1988, and though less frequently than before, he is still publishing.

For those familiar with it, this extensive œuvre constitutes an organic whole. Some basic qualities which go hand in hand with Weöres's poetic talent—his attraction to myth, transcendental and mystical interests, empathy, feeling for reality coupled with a pronounced inclination for abstraction, love of play and humour, the daring and persistence of his experimenting, a striving for the reconciliation of opposites, a serenity which raises him above the everyday world and, last but not least, an impressive linguistic and formal inventiveness —are the pillars on which the thematic arches of his work rest. Weöres's poetry is seemingly full of contradiction—it reveals its inner harmony and unity only gradually. The variety of themes, subjects, voices, the multiplicity of form and prosody, the virtuosity of language apparent even in this small

* Of these, I have used Zoltán Kenyeres's *Tündérsíp* (Budapest, 1983) in writing this introduction; I wish to express my thanks here.

selection are so impressively rich and unusual that the non-Hungarian reader surely needs some background information.

Weöres was born a year before the outbreak of the Great War on his father's 150 acres, that had been a 1,500-acre estate in his grandfather's time. It was here, in the countryside, that he learned the folk-songs, sayings, tales and games that were still prevalent at the time among the peasants. He became acquainted with poetry thanks to his mother and German governess. There was a local Theosophical Society, founded, like many others, during a visit by Annie Besant to Budapest in 1905, which in the poet's small village in time metamorphosed into an Anthroposophical Society, and his mother took the small boy with her to its meetings. Even decades later, the mysterious under-currents, the surrealistic march of bizarre disembodied beings, coupled with the other magically handled effects, helped to expand the field of vision of his poetry beyond the describable.

He was brought up a Lutheran, and his interest in the transcendental and metaphysical, and his attraction to mythology became apparent early. A history and anthology of Classical Antiquity in his parents' library started him on his way, and soon he also read Far Eastern philosophy, myths, and later, the medieval and modern Christian mystics. He was a poor student. At times he had a private tutor, at others he was sent from school to school in western Hungary. Yet even as a schoolboy he had impressive classical learning, and his perceptive teachers eased his way towards modern literature. Since the age of four or five he had been regularly writing verse, and this aptitude was coupled with an instinctive sense of form and inventiveness. Like a sponge, he soaked up the sound of folk-songs, and he also experimented, on the basis of his classical and modern reading, with variations on the poetic attitude, on the handling of his tools, imagery, condensation, linguistic and rhythmical shaping. Thus, poetically Weöres was mature at a truly Mozartian age; he wrote poems worthy of a poet, some of which are included in his collected works. His first appearance at the age of fifteen in a national daily caused quite a sensation. He first corresponded, then came into personal contact, with the major poets of the day, and soon his work was published in *Nyugat*, the coun-try's leading literary journal. One of the poems ("The Old Ones") he had published at the age of fifteen caught the eye of Zoltán Kodály, who set it to music; it became one of his most popular works for mixed choir.

But such early success so easily come by did not have an adverse influence on Weöres, who continued steadily on the road dictated by his talent. "The Old Ones" and "The Lunatic Cyclist", also included in this selection, are a good foretaste of the later works. In these he does not describe an experience or an episode. Leaving himself out of the poem, he describes his subject from a distance, focusing on the general or abstract—yet in a very concrete manner and sharply, as it were, placing it and, in the case of "The Lunatic Cyclist", the 'meaning' or 'message' of the grotesque is never spelt out, but is created by the reader. The sure handling of form and language is also impressive.

In 1933 Weöres started his studies at the University of Pécs in southern Hungary. Though there is no room here for a detailed study of the poet's development, mention must nevertheless be made of three great men who had a decisive influence on him. Karl Kerényi taught classical studies at the University of Pécs from 1934 on. Under the threat of Nazi propaganda, which even exploited Germanic mythology, the subsequently world-famous classical scholar, interpreter of myth and historian of religion emphasized the Mediterranean heritage, that spirit of the South which could serve as the basis of a modern Hungarian national consciousness as opposed to the false romanticism of the Asiatic steppes. Later, in Budapest, he edited a series under the title of *Sziget* (Island), which also had a strong influence on writers. In this he propagated the somewhat irrational and idealistic philosophical island idea, and tried to confront the barbarism of Fascism with an idealized Greek culture.

The philosopher and novelist Béla Hamvas, who also belonged to the *Sziget* circle and with whom Weöres became personally acquainted only in 1944, was the second strong influence on his thinking. Starting out from modern traditionalist philosophy, Hamvas began tracing the vanished world of the Golden Age, and collected and made use of those ancient texts which could serve as proof of the unity of existence or perfect harmony that was still present in ancient cultures. In this review of *Medúza* (1944), Weöres's fourth volume of poems, Hamvas encouraged Weöres to write Orphic poetry (this was a reference to Mallarmé) and to turn away from a poetry of outerness which had gained supremacy since the "Homeric straying from the true path," from superficiality, a fascination with the surface and from sensual enchantment. "In contrast, Orphic poetry is the true poetry which tames tigers and which makes fish raise their heads out of water." This encouragement was so much in line with Weöres's own inclinations and the direction of his experiments at the time that, after reading the review, he wrote to a friend: "Today's poetry by necessity can be no other but Orphic; in other words, it encounters reality not on the surface, not as phenomena, but only in the upper spheres; it must penetrate the substance of things, must experience things from the inside, must speak not *about* a thing, but must speak the *thing* itself. Or, rather, it shouldn't speak but sing, because man speaks *about* something and sings something."

The third person with a definitive influence on Weöres was the art historian and philosopher of art Lajos Fülep, teacher first at the University of Pécs, then for a short time at the Eötvös Kollégium in Budapest, where the intellectual élite was trained. Though in no way a radical, he was nevertheless neglected for most of his life. At the time Weöres met him, officially he taught history of art at the University while he was Calvinist minister of a nearby village. Weöres learned from him what it means to be a Hungarian in the European sense; he learned a modern, humanist ideal of culture and an approach to art based on philosophy. Even when he was an acknowledged poet, in fact until Fülep's death in 1970, Weöres always showed him his new poems first. Fülep was one of the most important intellectual touchstones and sources of inspiration to several generations of writers and artists, thanks not so much to his relatively small œuvre but to his charisma as a teacher. His influence can be compared only to that of the essayist and novelist László Németh and the Marxist philosopher Georg Lukács.

With his third volume, which appeared in 1938, Weöres had already taken an entirely independent direction, that of existence-expression instead of self-expression, the experimental road of the constant inherent in changing *phenomena*, that is not experience. He was searching for the unity between man and nature, the cosmos, in fact, the ennobling assurance of finality, gradually exiling the concrete self in all its forms from his poems. In his experiments he made use of every means at his disposal, from symbolism all the way to surrealism.

The result of Béla Hamvas's encouragement first took shape in a prose volume of brief pieces of wisdom, published in 1945. With its mixture of Oriental philosophy, pantheism, neo-Platonism, Christian mysticism and modern existentialism, it declared war on both individualism and all intentions directed at improving society. "Do not tolerate in yourself even the germ of any kind of intention to better society. For every generalized community is a fog; and he who runs about in the fog will sooner or later step on something living," says one of his teachings. The artist's escape from individualism does not point towards the world but towards uncommitted meditation which will lead to "love without feeling." "There is no good or bad in totality, there is no merit or mistake, no reward or punishment." "The home of science and art is not existence, the *esse*, but the possible, the *posse*, and if it is manifest in existence, it will make existence all the richer." Thus though the human condition, or life, may be hopeless, it can still be ennobled through art and creation. "There is something that is unchanging. The essence of everything is this unchanging thing. If I am freed of all incidentality, nothing of me will remain except the unchanging," says the "Summation" towards the end of the book.

This book appeared during the first awakening of a country in ruins, humiliated by the war, at the birth of the hope of a new age, and though in part it carried the trauma of war, with doctrines expressing in detail a social hopelessness and despair of a future, it met with general disapproval. In addition, Weöres's original poetic attitude was totally unlike what had been expected of a Hungarian poet throughout the centuries. Since the sixteenth century, history has shaped the fate of this nation, severed from Western Europe and not coming up to its own expectations, so that for want of the necessary institutions, a free press and so on, the cause of national independence, and social progress, or both, became the responsilibity of writers and poets. The great, eternal, universal subjects of poetry appeared, even in the works of the greatest, such as Petőfi and Ady, peculiarly entwined with the cause of the homeland and of progress. The poets centred around *Nyugat*, the generation before Weöres—specifically Mihály Babits, Dezső Kosztolányi and Milán Füst, who supported the young Weöres and whom he regarded as his masters until their death—were the first who dared to be poets, and could be great as such, without undertaking this role, though they never turned their back on the cause, and in their own way, outside of poetry, as men and writers, were part of it. Weöres turned away from it completely and explicitly. He was constitutionally unfit for the role.

Forging together his natural skills and the influences that acted on him, Weöres continued experimenting. Between 1945 and 1948, when he was silenced, four more volumes of his poetry were published. He had entered a critical stage of experimentation. In the early fifties, the time of Stalinism, when he wrote for his desk drawer and only his translations could be published, he was already a great poet at the height of his powers who had solved the problems of attitude and expression. In his experiments he made use of surrealism and dada, automatic writing, logical permutation, interprojection or superimposition, or else the floating of motifs living their own lives within the poem, daring games with rhythm, and an interaction of motifs and construction reminiscent of musical composition. In this volume, for example, his early poem "Homeward Bound" is an attempt at creating a fugue, while his "Symphonies" are large-scale 'musical' compositions with several movements, long songs at any rate in which the pronouncedly rhythmic, sometimes mysterious, almost melodious text—in Hungarian, at least—creates a definite musical, extra-verbal impression. Some of the choruses of "The Assumption", for example, are baroque and almost polyphonic in character; at other times the text is reminiscent of a chorale, a hymn, an anthem, or folk-song. But above all, after banishing the poetry of experience, the poetic Ego and the individual, and even going beyond modern objective verse, Weöres solved one of the most difficult problems of modern poetry, that of the expression of emotion. For this he needed the impersonal ancient, collective voice of myths, to create the impression that it was not the poet but, as it were, the consciousness of the world itself that was registering what is happening.

"The Assumption"—the "Seventh Symphony"—is outstanding not only in Weöres's work but in all of modern poetry. After the grave, seemingly detached images of mourning, relying on opposites, he presents the eternal, mystical themes of womanly existence, life, death, time, suffering, sacrifice, and love, in a manner which makes the poem emotional and rational, modern and ancient, deliberate and spontaneous, narrative and dramatic, gentle and cruel, grave and joyous, even exultant, all at the same time: philosophically abstract and sharply concrete in its imagery, but above all, spellbindingly evocative and suggestive. Going through a mysterious metamorphosis, the body turns into the source of life, and the assumption of the Virgin becomes the triumph of poetry which alone is capable of conquering death and calling forth the cosmic serenity and harmony indispensable for living. The brilliantly rendered, banal yet philosophical micro- and macro-story of "The Lost Parasol" radiates the same serenity as, following its slow decline and disintegration, this man-made utensil gradually returns to impassive nature.

The reader will notice that the present selection does not include poems from the seventies. At the time Weöres wrote an extensive and—by its very nature—untranslatable book, the complete works of an invented early nineteenth-century Hungarian poetess, Erzsébet Lónyay, whom he called Psyche: her verse, translations, personal notes and letters, complemented with a biographical study by one of her 'contemporaries' as well as the real text of a modern (real) critic, accompanied by a postscript relating the circumstances of the 'discovery' of this œuvre. Psyche, the adopted daughter of a count, was educated in a convent, but on her mother's side was a Gypsy, and therefore lived a life of extremes, full of adventure and amours, which in the language and poetic voice of the late rococo and early biedermeier she described with great honesty. She met Goethe, Hölderlin, Beethoven and the great Hungarian men of letters, and writes about her secret love affair with a (real) Hungarian poet of the age, just as she writes about every aspect of her feminine soul and the trivial events of her daily existence. Her life was cut short by a carriage accident; it is possible that her (justifiably) jealous husband, a Silesian land-owner, Count Maximilian Zeidlitz, had her put out of the way. The work is a *tour de force* on several counts. As pastiche, a brilliant linguistic game, it is so perfect that not even a stringent analysis could detect that the poems were not in fact written in the early nineteenth century. But the feat is multiple: thus Psyche sends her poems to the great critic of the age (who actually lived), who in his answer makes up a poem in the style of a contemporary (actual) poet. Weöres does not parody this poet, rather he writes lines as the great critic, who lived a hundred and fifty years ago and had nothing of the poet in him, would have written them. On another level, *Psyche* goes beyond the display of Weöres's empathy and love of games and turns into a feat of psychological transvestism as well. We experience the life, loves, maturation into a woman and later mother, the happiness and sufferings of a real woman. Going even further, as Zoltán Kenyeres writes in his above-mentioned book, *Psyche* "is the virtual creation of a life-style and a new possibility for life. The dream of a late rococo, early biedermeier literature in an independent and free Hungary, where poets are not burdened by the need to express the crucial problems of society and the nation but are free to devote themselves to the common manifestations of love, joy, and sorrow: this is the dream of a Hungarian literature, European in character, one that could afford the luxury of being Hungarian in language only and not necessarily in subject."

One of the secrets of Weöres's great popularity lies in the effect of the ribald poems and brilliant stylistic devices of *Psyche*, the other in the folk-song-like and humorous children's poems, sayings and short songs written with wonderful simplicity and magical poetic power. These fruits of experimentation with rhythm which Kodály encouraged, are known by hundreds of thousands, most of whom hear them first in kindergarten where they give them the first joyous taste of true poetry. These two aspects of Weöres are *ipso facto* untranslatable, and must remain Hungarian secrets.

The reader can judge better than I, what translation, which by its very nature flies in the face of providence, is capable of in the case of a poet who steers his poems from the ancient myths through the Far Eastern, classical and modern mystical philosophies all the way to the world of contemporary European man in the magnetic field of universal human culture, and does all this in Hungarian. I may have selected the poems for this anthology and have even participated in their translation, but like Weöres am Hungarian myself and know the poems in my native language. One thing is incontestable: there are first-class translations in this volume, which nevertheless means only that they provide an approach to, an approximation and glimpse of the original. I hardly know of any other poet in whose work form, rhythm, rhyme, linguistic invention and verse melody, all language-specific yet magical means which go beyond language and understanding and which touch the reader not in the sphere of the rational but at more ancient, more profound and sensitive spots, matter so much. All these are carriers of intangible content-defying meaning. On the other hand, there are also few poets in this century with so much imagination and power to make things manifest, who are able to see man and cosmos, life and death, microcosm and macrocosm, the material and the spiritual as an integral whole, making this magnificent vision shine forth with the serene harmony of real poetry, this greatest of human accomplishments.

MIKLÓS VAJDA

The Old Ones

They are so derelict, the old ones.

I watch them sometimes through the window
as they trudge home in an icy wind
with a back-load of firewood—
or in a panting summer
as they sit in the sunny porch—
or on winter evenings by the stove
slumped in deep sleep—
they stand in front of the church
with palms stretched out in sadness, downcast,
like faded autumn leaves
in the yellow dust.

And when they stutter through the street
with a stick, even the sunshine looks askance at them,
and everyone makes it sound odd to say:
"How goes it, old man?"

The summer Sun,
the winter snow,
autumn leaf,
crisp spring flower
all pour an endless song in their ears:
"Life-cauldronful of old meat,
life-cartful of old hay,
life-candleful of guttered wax:
you are eaten up,
you are thrown away,
you are burnt to nothing,
you can sleep now..."

They are like someone
ready for a journey
and starting to pack.

And sometimes, when their gnarled hands
caress the blond head of a child,
it must surely hurt them to sense
that these two hands,
hard-working hands,
blessing hands
are needed now by no one any more.

And they are already prisoners,
prisoners in chains, drowsy, apathetic:
seventy heavy years shackle their wrists,
seventy years of sin and grief and trouble,
seventy heavy years have chained them to wait
for a kindly hand,
a dreadful hand,
an unarguable hand
to give its command:

"Time now, lay it down."

[1928]   *Edwin Morgan*

The Lunatic Cyclist

sometimes one whose soul is pure
sees himself as if he might
be some cycling lunatic
as he pedals through the night

he the lunatic evokes
who can neither see nor hear
while the pebbles his wheels flick
are flung twanging through his spokes

wheels that cut into the earth
around him weave a dusty veil
the stars above a lazy herd
sleep in their narrow sky-stall

while the wind soaks up his sweat
and shakes out his bushy hair
the lunatic continues yet
to pedal through the moonlit air

sometimes one whose soul is pure
sees himself as if he might
be that lunatic cycling there
with mounting fury through the night

as clear to him as bread and wine
mirrored by the light of day
the moon that sprinkles round about
on every side its netted ray

cold the light and cold the wind
that blows the lunatic's hair back
while dust humiliates his wheels
and unvirginal is his track

———

infinite is the cyclist's track
and the soul that's pure and bright
watches while the lunatic
pedals weeping through the night

[1930]   *William Jay Smith*

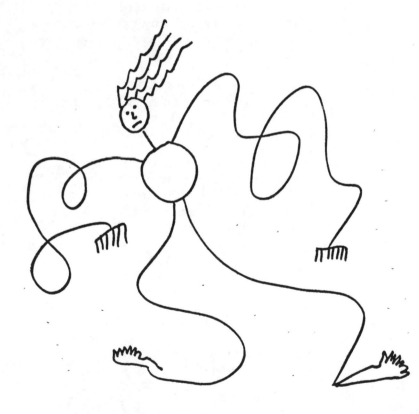

THE SPIRIT OF THE WIND

Eternal Moment

What you don't trust to stone
and decay, shape out of air.
A moment leaning out of time
arrives here and there,

guards what time squanders, keeps
the treasure tight in its grasp—
eternity itself, held
between the future and the past.

As a bather's thigh is brushed
by skimming fish—so
there are times when God
is in you, and you know:

half-remembered now
and later, like a dream.
And with a taste of eternity
this side of the tomb.

[1935]   *Edwin Morgan*

Homeward Bound

At the city-limits market
dark-green wreaths in a basket:
it is All Souls' Day today.
My life and death lie elsewhere,
the poem flies me home there,
to Csönge hamlet far away.

There, death is a dear relative:
a crypt stands as the family grave,
a guardsman, vigilant, steadfast.
A cool wind ruffles its grass-hair—
and its angles and its door
have ivy coats thickly massed.

The gathered clan of that one blood
floats with the plenum-seeking flood
like a galley in the moonlight:
my poor uncle Géza, and my
grandfather: men of mild eye
who nursed their trees up to the light.

What a crowd of layered coffins,
set down each on each, crosswise,
short or long, but in repose,
my stillborn younger brother who
had neither name nor life to rue,
my grandmother, my aunt Rose.

And great-grandparents and who knows
how many dowagers, airy girls,
ladies, artless child-angels—
under the vaulted stone they float
on their lovely backs as in a boat,
facing the sky's wide ranges.

Oh the minutes I stand here now,
oh the years I shall sleep below,
and I have never entered yet.
Here my millenniums will be spent,
here I must lie till the Judgement,
unloosed, dissolved, dispersed.

With an outsider's blood I escape,
but the omphalos is my trap,
back into the family pit.
All our breaths go down to it,
the living send root after root
into the chill, the inert.

I feel the steady breath of the crypt:
no ego, only family unit,
on individual judgement-throne,
and I am moved to recognize
ancestral habits as they revive
in the body I thought my own.

Pang of a moment in my fate:
what good is it for heart to beat
or morning blaze so dazzlingly?
The merely passing being goes,
I sing a happy song with those
hosts of the at-one-with-me:

"The space-stuff peeled off from us,
our being was gone, reason, like gas
from a puny puffed-up burner.
But what we have of interdependence
was born with eternity and is endless
through past present and future.

"Here the 'I, you, he' are one,
our sacred flock is mass-undone,
no walled-round being, everything streaming.
Our past deeds leave a churning wake
down through the years without a break
in a world left dreaming.

"We walked once on forbidden ground
and yet our trespass still praised God,
everything was from him, for him.
O Will that spurns a crude restraint,
forgive yourself in our old taint,
as your son promised when he came."

My wishes are: when I am dead
you must lay me in the bed
of our vault, just as of old.
Let some far descendant plough
my loamy knot of bones right through
dear Csönge's furrow and fold.

[1935]   *Edwin Morgan*

For my Mother

Rich teeming branch, you,
mother of mine,
my life's very first
woman,

big warm flower-bed,
soft pillow,
goblet brimming with
dawn-dew,

within you I found my
first nest,
my breast beat with
your breast,

between I and not-I no
barrier hung,
within you I and the world
were one.

My dream noses back into your
creeks and bays—
my dream noses back into your
creeks and bays!

Idol of alabaster,
mother of mine,
my life's titanic
woman,

your eyes gleam Isis-emeralded,
clear and fine,
your hair is bronze, Pallas-helmeted,
with pristine shine,

only on your face all shadows
grew hard,
like the hard afternoon sky
kestrel-barred.

My first beautiful toy,
mother of mine,
my childhood's opulent
woman.

The adolescence you gave me
got me mixed,
my eyes sidled from yours
unfixed.

I wondered: "Why did she give me
life and love
with nothing to be the eternal
life of?

I make her kill and bury
so much, I know!
Why did she not expose me
in the snow!"

The adolescence you gave me
got me mixed,
my man's heart found you again,
steady, fixed,

my man's heart found your heart,
your breast,
grateful now for minutes, years
and death.

My dream drifts back into
your arms,
my dream drifts back into
your arms...

Strong home, beautiful flag,
mother of mine,
my fate's unshakable
woman.

Once this whole life is squeezed in me
right through,
I will die into the all-in-all
as into you.

[1937]   *Edwin Morgan*

On Death

Don't mind if you die. It's just your body's shape,
intelligence, separate being, which are passing.
The rest, the final and the all-embracing
structure receives, and will absorb and keep.

All incidents we live through, forms we see,
particles, mountain-tops, are broken down,
they all are mortal, this condition shown,
but as to substance: timeless majesty.

The soul is that way too: condition dies
away from it—feeling, intelligence,
which help to fish the pieces from the drift

and make it sicken—but, what underlies,
all elements that wait in permanence,
reach the dear house they never really left.

[1937]   *Alan Dixon*

To the Moon

Moon, drifting on the dense foam of shimmering green
among easy veils, like a breath-clouded mirror,
while the stars of your great overarching sky are
    scurrying around you,

O you aimless big body, hovering and
waving lacy wings, harbouring no seed,
what dreams pilot the tedious seas of your
    primordial solitude?

Marvellous veiny stone! big round sky-gem!
non-transitory majesty! does the tiny sacrificing
of the living mortals that yearn toward your being
    ever reach you?

You magnetize the glad mad dog that lifts
his muzzle, his tail between his legs, and
howls his long-drawn Arab supplication;
    crickets in meadows

roll out their song for you like silver homespun;
and the human heart, when you beglamour it,
shines icily like a decaying birch tree and
    unravels into shadow.

Desireless satiety, high heavenly fiat,
you are praised by the least nocturnal whisper.
And our tiny sacrificing that yearns towards your being:
    does it ever please you?

Secretly you set up your dome over all lust,
you have salves to mollify the blaze of our torment,
and you sleep, and brilliant vacancy girds you,
    inertly loving.

[1938]   *Edwin Morgan*

from the *Sixth Symphony*

THE CONSTANT IN THE CHANGING

The earth flies fast, the old shag bird. And now, as it turns
on autumn nights, progressively withdrawing its north face
                                                    from light,
we may feel the fan of its wings as, ever faster, it furrows
the furthest pleats of space.
If you have seen much, speak: what is space hiding?
A vastness of unbodied arches, our latest brains reply,
springing its awful vault among infinities of light years,
pierced blindly by the stars—while we, stumbling on its veins
                                                    and fibres,
opening tiny windows, stare amazed at night,
that massive crown rests on no forehead,
and its inhuman radiance touches us.

But I know another space—more human
and even more mysterious. Just watch:
if you shut your eyes, where light has stabbed, the wound
continues boiling for a few more seconds,
the colours reversed, a hedgerow of blotches,
then washed away, your closed eyes project a dark space only,
like a vaulted hall, you cannot tell how large,
now small and reassuring, now immense, although it never
                                                    changes,
and a flame leaps in it sometimes, near or far, who knows,
and a soothing or a terrifying face,
and memory's faint skeletons come flying,
and miracles, those creatures of glass, fanning.
—I say: an inner space, unbreached by any speck of the tangible,
where nothing can be measured or has order,
where all is magically nascent, flitting, evanescent.

The space out there and that within us flood
and merge; this minute is a gift:
an open autumnal window where a tart breeze hesitates,
then streams in with the tang of mouldering stump-wood,
subdued carillons in the fog, like violins,
and you can guess the metallic scent of stars.
A pergola spins to the sky,
half mist-light, half thought,
a thousand flowers of creepers twine,
slender-pale and round-eyed little girls,
all different but you see the common sign:
their garments shaped by one care, one design.

Deeper than care nesting in your heart,
under the crust of each distinctive thing,
the basin of phenomena,
the hinges of the world are glistening,
the flame whirls in its vortex, the animated fire,
the thousand-eyed, spins on unshored,
drubbing of horses, sweating and battering,
their lathered haunches scintillate,
you hear their hooves' metallic clattering,
the element whistling at your ear is thin,
the infinite is tapping at your skin
and sizzles and grows a pellicle
like molten steel on ice.
It calls you—do you dream it? If you could wake to seeing
nothing alien in it nor cold
but a living wave of love, unscrolled
and closer kin to you than your own being!

[1938–39]   *George Szirtes*

Notes from a Diary

For some time now I've felt it stirring in me:
I resent having to share life, my good.
I, who once gave all things away gladly,
now find a miser lurking in my blood.

You come: I wine and dine you, but he weeps
and howls within me, calling my gifts back.
Deep in my heart this frazzled creature creeps
and wolf-like lopes beside a forest track.

But what have I, a dweller in holy lands,
to do with the vulgar world of material?
Desire does not request, it howls demands.
My soul goes pale and trembles at its call.

This author is ambitious to retire
from sensuous life, and bid the world adieu
when unattached at last, without desire
he might render unto other men their due.

Like one who builds a palace for the Lord
he hears a sudden rumbling from the deep;
and underneath the flagstones through the flawed
parquetry, the damp soil starts to seep.

I must confess, though repetition palls.
I've tried to build this shrine, but it won't hold.
The fountain presses through, and through the walls
the water pumps, the hot jets and the cold.

[1940]   *George Szirtes*

35

Self-Portrait

My friend, you who claim to know me,
look round my room: nothing of its decoration
was my own choosing; open my wardrobe:
it has nothing to show you that is specially me.

My lover and my dog know how I caress them,
but I remain unknown to them. My old instrument
is well aware of my hand's contours;
it too cannot sing about me.

Yet I am not in hiding—simply, I do not exist.
I act, I suffer, as all men do,
but my essential core is non-existence itself.

My friend, you must not regard me as having secrets.
I am as transparent as glass—how then
do you imagine you can really see me?

[1940]   *Edwin Morgan*

The First Couple

"Get up, Kukszu,
up, Kukszu, Kukszu, get up,
take your rod and thrash the trees!"

"I won't get up, Szibbabi, I won't get up,
my head lies heavy in scalding mud, my eyes
are shut, my face looks up to the sky,
I will not take my rod in my hand, Szibbabi, I will not
get up,
I am sending blood-red rain on you,
I am staying where I am."

Szibbabi went off,
when she got to the lake
lifted her apron.

"Lake frog, take a rod,
thrash the trees!"

"I won't trash, Szibbabi, I won't thrash the trees,
I live with my own true mate,
we hide from the hungry bird,
we eat big mosquitoes day after day."

Szibbabi let her apron down,
the blood-rain overtook her.

The frog smiled tenderly and said:
"Beyond the lake, beyond the mountains
there are twelve big-navelled gods
so fond of fruit, so fond
of mash, mash made with lard,
and they hold suckling babies in their laps,
and in their hip-bones they hold the world,
in their hip-bones both sky above and earth beneath,
and between these the water runs up and down."

———

Szibbabi left
by the lake-side, to get to the mountain,
over the mountain, to get to the twelve gods.
When she'd put the lake behind her
her head broke off from her neck,
rolled back into the lake.
When she'd got to the mountain
her trunk broke off at the waist,
lay there with her two arms.
When she'd found the twelve gods
then her two legs broke off.

The twelve gods smiled tenderly and said:
"You under the waist,
you above the legs,
you sack of skin once called Szibbabi,
let the blood-rain leave you,
may you shut as tight
as shell round ripening seed,
and when the new light spills over
let out your young, be flat again,
become a cracked and juiceless skin,
and let your young be Kukszu."

Kukszu sprawls in scalding mud,
head in silt, feet in sedge,
face turned to the sky,
sends no more blood-rain into the body of Szibbabi,
cries with sharp call, a suckling child,
waiting for the overflowing light, for the overflowing light
waiting, for the never-returning light.

[1941]   *Edwin Morgan*

De Profundis

Whatever my origin, driven out into the earth,
my clothes will always carry the sheepfold stench
    of things here below.
This is the place where God's every plant and beast
pullulates through its appalling feast,
    chewing its neighbours raw.

I confess it was not good I expected to find,
but such a freight of misery was far from my mind:
    a son of a different star,
if he had even one minute's taste of our pain,
plunged into molten ore with sparks like rain,
    would soon be steam and air.

We swing from keen to glum, from gloom to joy,
up and down, up and down in our seesaw,
    swung without a say,
like someone forced by torturers to watch
a strobe of light and dark until they hatch
    his madness in that way.

Any reason in this world is a poor by-blow of Reason,
scrabbling at the mere shell of things, seizing
    nothing near the bone.
Half-asleep in half-darkness we slump,
wrestling through our fray in the deep swamp,
    our prison and our home:

for what are we but cannibals of each other,
buying our own life with the death of a brother:
    earth's law, earth's fee.
What are brothers but stone, tree, beast, man,
I eat my brother with gut-slithering pain,
    and my brother eats me.

An alley cat laps a young chick's blood:
one twists in death, one fights for food:
    I suffer both the same.
Rocks are crushed, earth's flesh punctured, cut:
neither stone nor earth knows any hurt,
    but I have the pain.

When anything is killed, I am killed,
the earth with all its miseries and ills
    gapes me its jaws.
A fly hits a flame: I'm writhing there,
I'm dying a thousand times every hour
    and without a pause.

Split the veil into the next existence,
and I shall still look shivering down the vistas
    and pits of this world.
There would be no assuaging even in heaven:
God's own light will build no haven,
    nor my lament grow cold.

[1942]   *Edwin Morgan*

Fragment

My lips, my teeth will perish: but my laughter will not die!
My brow, my eyes will dry out: but my weeping will not die!
because my members are all separate, but my laughter and my
                                                    weeping
are one and the same thing: not to be counted among dualities,
all things embraced in it like an island in the twin forks of a stream,
sifting and sifted, trickling through what perishes.
My laughter and my weeping are not me, nor am I my clothes,
for you though heaven clothes me in seamless, frayless garments.
My hands hold nothing finished—I could well be mournful,
on earth though where all sorrow begets sorrow: I don't want to be
                                                    mournful
I could abandon fortune's wheel—I could indeed be happy,
on earth though, here where live things feast on live things: I don't
                                                    want to be happy
I don't know where I come from, no more than you know where
                                                    you come from
but here on earth I live now and carry the burden with you.
I don't know if I desired to come here, driven by pity or passion,
but here I am and my whole being yearns to bear the burden.
I come like an ass laden, not questioning his cargo,
and when I leave you all I shall be as frayed and lightless as a rag.
But my laughter and my weeping shall not fray: eternal and
                                                    identical the pair,
to tend you while they cast me off and crush me.
And later, when you cross time's nether threshold their single
                                                    shape conjoined
will stand there and will greet you, like one who knows you and
                                                    whose work is finished.

[1942]   *George Szirtes*

The Underwater City

Who has no crumbling smoke—who has buried
all her flowers among the sad deaf waves, afraid
of the evil and for its sake shunning the good as well:
coward-city! she stirs my heart.

Instead of the sheet of the sky
the living sheet of seaweed, covering,
moving endlessly, noiselessly, mum as a thousand mice.
Noiseless seaweed music, thinkable music, not for the ear,
bygone city music, once heard by the ear—
musicless in this place the underwater city.

This city too I will throw off, till nothing is left.
Let her swim in the abyss of my past, waving her seaweed-cover,
lamenting her flowers and her bygone music.
Her cairn of stones, like knee-pans of scrawny gods,
their hard hip-bones and rasping ribs,
is beyond anxiety: death seizes, fuses everything.
Because I cast even this coward-city off, I want no memories of
                                        the music either.
Even her melancholy seaweed-cover is too much for me.

And if someone comes and asks me what I have:
what have I gathered in this world among
the monotonous mechanical clatter of nights and days?
what gives me licence to spend or hoard?—
I will show him this city. Rejected infernal city!
Look now: dying stones, flowers desired,
old trembling through the seaweed—such is the underwater city.
Yet I say: this is all you can gather together.
Because there is nothing more anywhere.

[1942]   *Edwin Morgan*

Wedding Choir

1

Life-filled longing of the buoyant smile strains against
imminent certainty, against the radiant food-bringer.
Brooding between good and evil, it loses bright warmth in languor,
slips down blood-red below empty stars, into chequered mutilation.
But the white bird of Union flies to it, nestles there,
settles maturely, hugely, in the flashing joy of the message.

2

Flocks of bright fables rise over the spreading scarlet cinders:
dead skeleton and growing body are praised by the greybeard.
A cart, where troubled charm and trancelike beauty warm
        themselves wound into one,
painful and shining, like plunging into sleep: close to the cauldron
        is the feast of the fable.
Kingfisher-flocks fly shrieking: the cry links everything!
the ritual fire flashes: prophecy pours time in its mould.

3

The straining pillar and the dancing fire are obstinate as a
        marriageable girl:
unsignalled instantaneousness, little sailing half-moons,
veiled smile and stunned gladness, fading like the colour of flowers,
brilliant caprices that instead of hurting brim over with love.
Long the street, but a thousand lodgings on both sides harbour
        saintly unity.
Seed of all things: clear dignity! and sweet the broken fortune
        piercing the husk.

4

The tense wing crumples, the glimmering laughter burns out,
shadow looms, and the steady pulse of hunger beats to its quietus.
Between good and evil, in colourless mist, a dim ripple of the soul,
the desperate slopes and huddle of stars adrift in it.
The Shining Fish lives, a peace unbroken,
an ambergris-scented order, clothed with imperfection and
        salmon-running joy.

[1944]   *Edwin Morgan*

To Die

Eyes of mother-of-pearl, smell of quince,
voice like a bell and far-off violins
and hesitant steps hesitating, thickening,
heavy-horned twins of emptiness snickering,
sinking, cold brimming, blue wide over all!
Wide magnet blue, ploughs flashing on,
and burning thorns in naked storm,
earth-wrinkles, dropped on pitted soil,
shaking the wild sweet nest, the bright
dish flying in its steady-spread light.

[1944]   *Edwin Morgan*

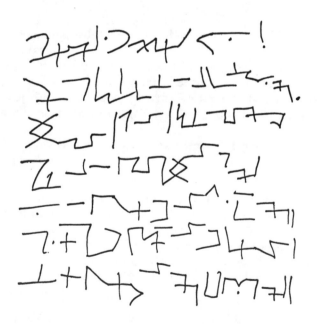

POEM IN A SECRET LANGUAGE

'Eternal darkness clings...'

Eternal darkness clings to the concave of the surface.
That is the ingrown frame
of things; that is hell. Uniform the night-face,
uninterruptedly stony, black, unflickering flame.

That is hell: life tilts out from it, the
scatterer, out from this stillness! Clod, grass, man, animal,
all spring from it, all that hurt and kiss each other,
from hell, all those on whom sun-rays fall!

The outer and the inner arch of things—
is it obverse or reverse that rings?
is there a third arch: light without dark?

From soil to heart, all things sing;
not with intellect: they respond with their being,
like a woman, a poem, just as they are.

[1945]   *Edwin Morgan*

Whisper in the Dark

From a well you mount up, dear child. Your head a pyre, your arm a stream, your trunk air, your feet mud. I shall bind you, but don't be afraid: I love you and my bonds are your freedom.

On your head I write: "I am strong, devoted, secure, and home-loving, like one who wants to please women."

On your arm I write: "I have plenty of time, I am in no hurry: I have eternity."

On your trunk I write: "I am poured into everything and everything pours into me: I am not fastidious, but who is there who could defile me?"

On your feet I write: "I have measured the darkness and my hand troubles its depths; nothing could sink so deep that I should not be deeper."

You have turned to gold, dear child. Change yourself into bread for the blind and swords for those who can see.

[1946]   *Edwin Morgan*

The Colonnade of Teeth

1

The Colonnade of Teeth, where you have entered,
red marble hall: your mouth,
white marble columns: your teeth,
and the scarlet carpet you step on: your tongue.

2

You can look out of any window of time
and catch sight of still another face of God.
Lean out of the time of sedge and warblers:
God caresses.
Lean out of the time of Moses and Elias:
God haggles.
Lean out of the time of the Cross:
God's face is all blood, like Veronica's napkin.
Lean out of your own time:
God is old, bent over a book.

3

Head downwards, like Peter on his cross,
man hangs in the blue sky with flaring hair
and the earth trundles over the soles of his feet.
The one who sees
has sleepless eyes he cannot take from man.

4

No sugar left for the child:
he stuffs himself with hen-droppings and finds what's sweet.
Every clod: lightless star!
Every worm: wingless cherub!

5

If you make hell, plunge to the bottom:
heaven's in sight there. Everything circles round.

Man lays down easy roads.
The wild beast stamps a forest track.
And look at the tree: depth and height raying from it to
                                        every compass-point;
    itself a road, to everywhere!

Once you emerge from the glitter of the last two columns
the cupola your hair skims is then infinity,
and a swirl of rose-leaves throws you down,
and all that lies below, your bridal bed: the whole world—
Here you can declare:
"My God, I don't believe in you!"
And the storm of rose-leaves will smile:
"But I believe in you: are you satisfied?"

[1946]   *Edwin Morgan*

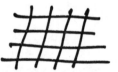

Megnyugvás a zárban

RESIGNATION IN CAPTIVITY

To a Skeleton Fastened
Together with Wire

You flesh-hatched statue, artifice of lace,
the slimy body's final dried-out station,
the clatter of your jaw as you are shaken
drums sacred rhythms, spins you to cleanliness.

This small excrescence who stands in for me
dotes not on you but incense, gold, some dead
beast for his table, hot damp games in bed.
Poor fool—he shares his spoils generously.

Clasp him to your ribs, he's like a state
strutting to what the *hoi polloi* dictate,
collapsing laurelled in his heap of silt.

The flesh is filth throughout, up to the hilt,
but you, bone man, are pure, stripped, ultimate;
the one flower of our being not to wilt!

[1946]   *George Szirtes*

Canzone

For my wife

I don't know yet how much you mean to me;
concerning you the soul thinks silence due
and draws round you a veil; I cannot see,
O love, as yet, what I am worth to you;
whether I'll bring you luck, or else, some day,
my death's jewel, gem and gold, I have no say
    at all, in honeyed sway
of a new pain's tendrils I could miss my way.

But all I know is a companion
has come, one never expected by my heart,
and taken life and death and in return
has brought into my forest another light;
a troop of birds and beasts of prey is fleeing,
clattering, made homeless by the lightning flame;
    I am afraid my shieling
may fall if you don't take it as your home.

But all I know is that my body has rested
familiar on your flexible body since
some long-lost time, and that my head is nested
there on your breast, that shameless tears convince
that I have nothing to hide, and you explore
my wild Tibet long years, knowing it well,
    unsteady pity or
questioning eye for what the stars can tell.

The nerve torn out, the screech-owl cast from grace,
will find in time the blue lamp of your eye;
your lap, little lady, is a hiding place
for the sleeping dog of sensuality;
inside, the King of Light, eternal man,
still silent, may not know your lovely name,
    and waiting does not claim
to judge, wearing for love his long pink gown.

[1947]   *Alan Dixon*

from the *Fifth Symphony*

THE SCARLET PALL

Your first dream—the dream just cradle-born—
two rosy children in naked interlace
eating each other, biting into soft fat flesh.

Second dream: the black sacrifice to your mother.
Lifting the stone lid, and silence out of the dark.

Third dream now: in shadows of furniture, in a corner
friends hanging head downwards in the air like
blinded lamps... who knows if they're alive...

　　Oh how endlessly
dream ripples out, washes in sullen folds,
clashing thread on scarlet ground: dream-star-army!
figures of lightning on the blood-red pall!

　　Remember yet:
the spearlike bud bursts from man's groin,
woman's groin unfolds its flower to meet it,
and as a bow touches a fine quivering string
the bud gushes into the offered cirque of petals.
　　Remember yet:
you roam over dead plateaux and rock-wrinkles,
you come upon someone buried to the chin in stone,
and both the roamer and the buried one are you yourself!
You stumble clumsily over the protruding head,
but the other head suffers the kick of your boots.

　　All your dream,
　　all mine too:
our child-dreams drink pearls at the same spring.

A heaven of lace on the rust-crusted outposts,
images on the scarlet pall! Branch-writhing dream!

———

Dance, dance,
swing through the distance:
what an initiation
your childtime night was!
and the cyclops-eye of the world sat on your skull,
its thousand faces flaked to the bone on your cot,
remember yet—

Across time and space
creep, creep to me:
our savage factious hearts have common root in the earth.
Common, what lies in wait for us.
Think: you are walking in smoke. Your eyes are bandaged.
Heat of torches hits you; you are led by the hand.
And soon perhaps, without fear,
you will sacrifice yourself:
the arch of your eye-covering tugs the flame inwards!
No hiding then from your blood-coloured pall!

[1946–51]   *Edwin Morgan*

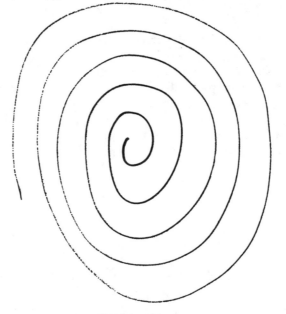

THE SMILING SNAIL

Signs

I

The whole world finds room under my eyelid.
God squeezes into my head and heart.
This is what makes me heavy.
This is what makes the donkey I sit on unhappy.

II

Heaven's crazy-man: light: you
pouring your face on the surface of the water,
what is that girl's face you proffer
stripping from your own madness?

Great saint, having swum through this world
you came to the empty silence, endlessness,
you climbed with the void to a crystal wedding-dress:
be frank, what woman is it like?

III

Man, waken the secret woman in you:
woman, light up your masculine state:
for if the Invisible embraces you,
it will enter you and take you into it.

IV

Oh how large then is love
if it goes with us in our whirlpools?
And what large love lies waiting in us
if it can be taken into our whirlpools?

V

More than your heart's cloudy afflictions,
more than your mind's labour of doubt—
value your toothache more than that,
for it shines out.

Your questions have only words as their answer,
but each thing answers itself.

[1947–48]   *Edwin Morgan*

from *Hymns of Ancient Times*

THE RAPE OF THE EARTH

A bushel of crabs, a calf's head
with protruding tongue, frozen eyes,
beneath it bacon beaded
in fat, with red-and-white undulating
streaks, one small bag of spices,
a strand of garlic and a young
rooster and hen, still lukewarm,
dangling on leather straps from his shoulder—
he then put down his load, sat down in a corner,
resting his coarse heavy fists on his knee
like someone who has brought a lot with him but does not want
to disturb anyone;
only his downcast, restless eyes kept circling. And the women
were not really bustling around him at all: they seemed to
indicate that
it was not the opulent newcomer but the young master who was
cherished here,
he who, blond, smiling and fragile,
lay next to the fireplace on his straw bed,
not yet suspecting anything. Only the bleary pap-eater,
the great-great-grandfather of them all, who had been alive from
the beginning
and had seen earth and water burst forth from nothing
and the stars pullulate like showers,
knowing that no one would listen to him anyway,
mumbled to himself: "It was like that then too—
a lot of food and drink opened the gate,
but no good came of it."—And the feast was readied:
in the place of honor the young master lay and
beside him, at his head his mother, at his feet his woman,
around him his sisters one after the other, and, at the end,
the opulent stranger who was both guest and host.

Their door stood wide open:
in the yard noon was shining,
bridal trees extended and
displayed their blessed branches;
a white horse went prancing by,
its colt hurrying behind it,
while inside gaiety broke loose in song; and the master-eye
did not notice that from afar, snakelike, stealthily,
a bushy, lumpish hand had reached over;
it caressed all his sisters, his mother, his woman,
from knee to hip. — Then at the cooling fireplace
the flame shot up for the last time and hid in the ashes,
the charred log gave off a final puff, its smoke wreathed in dirt.
By then the master was alone. Of a sudden
blood shot up into his head, his sight became blurred,
his throat glowed, hot and dry:
he ran to the sleeping quarters. His mother stood there in her shift,
his sisters peeped out, cuddling together, naked,
and there was the stranger, vintaging on the master-bed,
resting between the wet thighs of the young woman,
then he tore himself out like a stump from the earth. The young
                                              master reeled,
a rock-heavy hollow noise burst from his throat,
and, seeing that they had all pulled away and no one remained
                                              with him,
collapsed in the corner like a rag and wept there quietly.
And the old man, a witness since the beginning of time,
mumbled: "The same thing happened long ago;
it was just so when the Earthmother was raped
and that one came into the world of whom there is no deliverance."

[1949]   *William Jay Smith*

55

Clouds

In the mirror of the open window the mirror-cloud drifts facing the cloud. Cupids melt off at its edge, the heavy centre writhes with the lumbering bodies of monsters, a satiny blueness retracts and spreads bitten between gaping rows of beast-fangs. A violet coach flakes off, hurries away into the blue and quickly vanishes: yet it is easy to imagine it galloping there out of sight: gods are sitting in it, or the no-beings of non-being, or the dead we have heard the earth thudding down on and know nothing about any more.

The clouds drift and the mirror-clouds face them; and for anyone watching, nature drifts face to face with thought in the depths of his skull.

[1951]   *Edwin Morgan*

MAN AND HIS ENVIRONMENT

from *Orbis Pictus*

AN ENCOUNTER WITH NO ONE

In my dream you asked for a farthing and I gave you none.
I awoke: you never lived, I know.
But now I'd gladly give you a sovereign, no doubt about it,
but you gallop away too quickly down the road.

NOTHING

1

The sky is a complete barren blue sphere around me,
there is no solid earth anywhere, only a cord stretched out;
in gaping space I crawled out on that, then fell,
and now am plunging direction-less and alone.

2

"Because light shines on my face, I can see through closed eyes,"
whispers the goddess on the pillow,
"seven torches burn, I sleep in brightness;
you watch the curve of my lips to learn what I am dreaming of."

3

A hole is singing. Through lamplight,
behind streets, a hole is singing.
With blessed rage, its back to all that is visible,
it answers all things that have not come into existence.

CONCEPTION

Men and women were sporting themselves in the city.
As a dream-coil, I flew past them.
Their warm fumes drew me, clung to me,
and I became an earth-son, a prisoner, in a womb.

BIRTH

When a child is born, a window is red.
On the other shore of being, someone is dead
and already shrieking: while behind him roll
the waxen rivulets of grief and dread.

THE SENTIMENTAL TYRANT

Genghis Khan returns home, the father of five,
leaving robbery and genocide far behind,
he weeps for his canary with its broken leg
and keeps watering the lilies in his garden.

TURNING POINT

For a thousand years I stuffed a sack with shadow
to purchase the hilltop from the lake-mirror.
Then when I emptied the sack, only a finch's
leg was missing. What is the point?

THE DIARY OF THE PAST

1

O the light flag of the future!
Anything may be expected—salvation, damnation.
O the embossed coffin of the past!
Of the many things, one happened: always the same.

2

Everything is but the cheap imitation image of itself,
for it crumbles away, leaving not even a memory behind;
but just look into the benumbed ice-ocean of the past:
every movement is there, hardened into place.

3

You can blow away a house and a mountain-top
sooner than a single feather reduced to ashes yesterday.
Things show their eternal face
in the past. Existence does not alter them.

PRAE-EXISTENTIA

God has been thinking you throughout eternity;
in his brain your being stands out like a rock.
What is your foam-bubble of life compared to that?
And does your death alter you at all?

EXISTENTIA

I awaken: I am not the one I was.
I fall asleep: tomorrow I will be different again.
But alive, dead, in the street, in the crypt,
it is I who remember and forget.

POST-EXISTENTIA

You will not rest, dead or alive, until
you have rewoven your color and shadow
into the handwoven infinity of love;
peace will only then be yours.

FAREWELL

1

What can I give you? Almost nothing: advice.
Of all the thousands of fates I cannot step
into yours, while the abyss awaits you, yawning,
to protect you even from your self.

2

What your desire demands: go out and steal it for yourself;
what your being demands: is there, laid out in abundance.
Only illusion remains ever thirsty;
reality does not yearn for drink.

3

Whatever your wickedness, your foolishness,
it does not even brush your pure depth.
When your fabric and crust have peeled off,
love will stand out like a bare cliff.

[1952]   *William Jay Smith*

The Assumption

SEVENTH SYMPHONY

To the memory of my mother

I

The shadow, the stone, the linen, the lime,
the cushion beneath the cranial arch,
Death's swaddling clothes, Death's iron lock
the clods that coldly clatter down;
while still the body-shadow climbs
higher than ultimate flame can dart
and, rotting, the sweatband pries the earth apart.

Feet from striped sheets protrude;
cold wax wraps the clotted veins,
purple bathes exposed toenails.

The bound legs now stretch out at ease:
sinews are straightened, unflexed the knees;
along the rock path, olive trees.

Hail to thee, O withered womb.
The armored beetle, through a crack in the wall,
scrapes the cliff's edge and lets fall
his bristling pennants and his lance.

Hail to thee, hands clasped in prayer,
votive candles in their arching shrine,
candles melting in a double line,
ten swan-wings dipped in evening dew,
closed blossoms of the flowering night.

Hail to thee, heart-of-seven-swords,
whose painful cry we hear descend,
dropped stone-encased in a fathomless well,
since time's beginning to no known end.

Narrow neck, tilted head, hair stuck down,
white face with the leaden penny of the last ransom,
the cool cast of the senses' wrinkles
around the mouth-slot and the sunken eyes;
the twisted twigs of the trampled acanthus,
and the prints of steeds that have charged away.

Shadow, night,
silence, cold,
creaking, snapping,
dark clods falling,
light rays cleaving,
dust motes singing,
high above, two
new moons at their apogee,
fiery net down-reaching
with spider-legged embers
released ever upward,
wings beating slowly
on peaks white and gleaming,
flocks of sheep waiting,
harps and flutes playing,
violins wailing,
belfry bells clanging,
brasses replying;
from ashes our forebear,
a long time now faceless,
bones now assembling,
features all golden,
leans on one elbow,
and, risen to full height,
hears now these voices:

Chorus

Her shrill call goes out, out, out
to loved ones in darkness:
tending flocks in the starlight,
with her baby, we saw her.
In springtime, while shearing,
in winter we skinned hides,
with mounds of white fleece, in blue water-mirror,
with clouds floating outward,
we swam with the clouds:

when our boat
touched shore,
she saw
who we were,
thorn-shredded,
our sandals;
earth-stained,
our foreheads.
Shepherds we are but sheep we are also:
quick to our shearing,
and quick to our skinning;
let us cover her path with our hides.
To loved ones in darkness
her shrill cry goes out.

3

Alternating choruses

Double oars drumming
bright infinite silence,
froth-steam of breath, pale purple
foaming against the white dazzle,
whirled masts unfurling,
armadas set swirling,
mist-bridge, gold barge,
flame-ferry, fever's reverse side
mirrored in diamond,
far-off rings and ripples,
enraptured children rushing,
tears welcoming a rainbow,
veined shimmer of milk-foliage,
womanhood fêted over the world.
    (Whereas we always wept;
    we were forever starving.
    What else could we do?
    We always wept.)
. . . her wake all aglitter in surging foam,
on the moon's yellow crescent,
on the earth-eye's giant blue cataract,
on the chariot's red wheels,

on the comb of the green monster,
on the black mouth-cavity of cold—
and in the evening she will make your white bed
and follow you through hell;
and when the nest breaks up, call you back.
    (Upturned stumps,
      roots growing upward,
      the soil has ejected us;
      no one will bend down to us.)
. . . inside you she kneels, and you will become her,
if you lay down your bridal wreath, my love,
from which roses draw their color and your eyes their light;
and you sense her presence when you hide your chalice,
from which, flaming-hot,
drank abysmal mist-creatures,
and numbered centuries
with rage-marked foreheads. . .
    (Flowers worm-infested—
      who needs a torn petal,
      while spring morning showers down?)
. . . ever-waxing moon of rising vision,
fluttering upward from half-darkness,
aroma, thickening under the fruit skin,
and bursting into flame in the hidden veins,
below the heart, within a warm arbor,
star-crowned, royal dream,
grape cluster dripping hot red wine:
the mother's flame burns over the world. . .
    (Whom did I kill? Always myself.
    Whom does it hurt? Me.
    Leave me in peace in the womb.)
. . . slender hands curved in prayer,
taut pillars of grace,
mist-roofed fingers,
mother-winged living silence,
naked fingers in a sea of petals,
tenfold resonance that is soundless,
giving off a glitter that is beamless,
a clarity uncharted as a kiss. . .
    (The salt of sweat in our bread,
      the taste of death in our meat;
      coffin walls enclose us.)

... she who stood below the cross
and did not succumb in agony
gazes at the cresting foam of the cross
with startled clear-blue child eyes
and weeps on the threshold of hell
while in their foul dens the dead,
cloaked in guarded night,
blink in the wounding light...
   (Remove the poison from our hearts down-dripping,
    the black maggot,
    the live coals, the darkness—
    remove from our hearts.)
... that blue-eyed radiance
cuts through all currents;
the arching band of space mirrors it—
time, flashing, many-channeled, also reflects it:
a sweet drop on a nodding reed,
a radiant, changing globe,
it grows, eternally spinning off—
the virgin's peace floats through the world...
   (Trembling with cold, we draw our cloaks closer;
    have mercy on us, Our Lady.
    Pray for us,
    have mercy on us.)

4

Over the fountain
from spread wings
feathers whirl, snow falls;
in great vats
new wine ferments;
on balconies
hosts gather
a thousandfold;
the earth's chained
wrath is silent;
air fills
with wing-sound.

Chorus

Through light, through flame
moves dark earth's virgin;
never have shadow and darkness
cracked open
more fiercely
with the dance of vision
over hill and valley;
by a siege-chain of twined flowers
that give a wasteland new color.

Vein-of-the-rose, blood-of-the-turtledove,
chalice brimming with mild sour-cherry wine,
deep-reaching hill shadow,
hope ever-harvested,
blood-pearl of snowbound chamois roe,
summoning the hunter to a steep incline,
where the path is narrow, the space wide.
Sweet mother, young bride,
delicate red-cheeked daughter,
our rippling wings reach to you,
a sea of frilled swaying;
will you fly to us? Will you gaze upon us?
Our bodies carpet your path,
soft springtime, sweet mother.

Mary

I praise Him, conceived in my womb,
who raised my crescent moon,
who with stars garlanded my forehead
and caused my train to sweep along the Milky Way,
my veil to be blown by gusts of sweetness,
and my chariot propelled by radiant fires,
with hosts thronging my triumphal procession,
building towers of eternal song around me;
so He has wished: and raging armies, dark generations,
revolving under my pleated steps,
cannot comprehend this.

From the beginning my father—and I bore Him—
who through the giant void,
above the scintillating crystal of silence,
above the swirling current of creatures,
towers, a triple-headed column;
and, a three-pronged flashing roof,
the halo of the triple forehead protects me.

Chorus

O Queen of bluebells,
converging before you,
bell-hearts beating in a thousand bodies,
rayed-dome swaying,
mist-tower quaking,
for you we toll, to you we confess;
if our bells are rough-cast,
silence us, O Queen.

Mary

The judgement is not mine: the scales, the axe
are not in my hand: I never learned to strike
but only to stroke; never to starve but only to feed,
never to wound but only to be wounded; never to take but
only to ask;
in the nameless void, in the resonant silence
habits and bridal gowns flourish upon me;
lion and kid share my breast.
The babe soils me but leaves no stain;
he scratches my breast and a rosary of blood-drops issues forth;
the swelling sea does not feel its lack.
I wipe off the blood the murderer spurts on me;
revile me and I do not turn away.
Stone wall I am not, to measure strikes and strokes
as they are measured against it;
clay road I am not, to measure steps and turns
as they are measured out upon it;
fountain of fire I am not, to reflect body and void
looming before it:

I am but a nest, but being warm, I warm.
You who see me triumphant in glory,
consider: that glory comes not from me.
As with you, my only treasure is my tears;
my son's wound is my boundless domain,
the misery of this world my gateless garden.
In my lap is the thick-leaved tree of life;
and if you break off from it and sink under it,
your wilful fist will grasp my apron
and you will lay the stump of your head on my knee.
Fear not: my tears and my silence will protect you.

Chorus

Below, in the lightless deep,
at the base of the nightingale's nest,
thorn-bound hearts grow
in a vast forest thick with sighs;
planets revolve with new destinies,
but those eternally smiling slumber in peace,
their mouths honey-tipped.

Below, a rose-bush full-blooming;
on the hill pink dawn breaks:
weakness and strength,
with shared fingers, offer a feast
a residue of ashes on the hearth
but purple floods the gray depth,
announcing eternal dawn.
Soft-swaying field of roses,
flame breathing in the wind,
by radiant eyes spellbound,
she draws near, her train revolving slowly behind her;
a rose-sea of waving infants
reaching after her:
death stands still, time is suspended.

Change tautens
like a string:
ancient embers
again heat up;
dark from the grave,
the patriarch
drones to himself
the word fulfilled;
liplike the clods
are now stuck shut;
eternal the sound
of opening wings.

Coda

Mary, woman of star paths,
protect Mary, my mother,
while she pursues her path,
torn forever from my sight.

You who have heard these words,
a splinter of the song
that pierces the world's heart,
you who have heard these words, awake
and leave those monsters asleep beside you.

[1952]   *William Jay Smith*

The Lost Parasol

*I think there is much more in even the smallest creation
of God, should it only be an ant, than wise men think.*
ST TERESA OF AVILA

Where metalled road invades light thinning air,
some twenty steps more and a steep gorge yawns
with its jagged crest, and the sky is rounder there,
    it is like the world's end;
nearer: bushy glade in flower,
farther: space, rough mountain folk;
    a young man called his lover
    to go up in the cool of daybreak,
they took their rest in the grass, they lay down;
the girl has left her red parasol behind.

Wood shades sunshade. Quietness all round.
What can be there, with no one to be seen?
Time pours out its measureless froth and
    the near and the far still unopened
    and midday comes and evening comes,
no midday there, no evening, eternal floods
that swim in the wind, the fog, the light, the world
and this tangle moves off into endlessness
like a gigantic shimmering silk cocoon,
skirted by wells of flame and craters of soot.

Dawn, a pearl-grey ferry, was drifting
    on its bright herd of clouds,
from the valley the first cow-bell came ringing
and the couple walked forward, head by head;
    now their souvenir clings to the shadows,
red silk, the leaves, the green light on it, filtering,
    metal frame, bone handle, button:
    separate thing from the order of men,
    it came home intact, the parasol,
its neighbours rockface and breeze, its land cold soil.

In a sun-rocked cradle which is as massive
as the very first creation itself
        the little one lies, light instrument
on the blue-grey mossy timber of a cliff,
around it the stray whistling, the eternal murmuring
of the forest, vast Turkey-oak, slim hornbeam,
briar-thickets, a thousand sloe-bushes quivering,
noble tranquil ranks of created things,
and among them only the parasol flares out:
jaunty far-off visitor whose clothes still shout.

        Languidly, as if long established there,
            its new home clasps it about:
the rocks hug their squat stonecrops,
above it the curly heliotropes
            cat's-tail veronica,
wild pinks push through cage of thistles,
dragon-fly broods on secret convolvulus,
dries his gauze wings, totters out:
so life goes on here, never otherwise—
a chink in the leaves, a flash of blue-smiling skies.

        The huge-lunged forest breathes at it
            like yesterday, like long ago,
mild smell of the soft nest of a girl.
        Shy green woodpecker and russet
frisky squirrel refused to sit on it,
who knows what it hides: man left it;
but a nosy hedgehog comes up to the ledge,
the prickly loafer, low of leg,
like a steam puffer patrols round the rock;
puts heart in the woodpecker tapping at his trunk.

        The sun stretches out its muscular rays:
you would expect the bell of heaven to crack.
Broad world—so many small worlds find their place
in you! Through the closed parasol's hills and valleys
an oblong speck moves: an ant that drags
the headless abdomen of a locust with rapt
persistence and effort: up to the bare heights,
down to the folds, holding the load tight,
and turning back at the very end of the way,
floundering up again with the body. Who knows why?

This finger-long journey is not shorter or sillier
than Everything, and its aim is just as hidden.
Look: through the branches you can see the hillside,
there a falcon, a spot on the clear sky,
hangs in the air like a bird of stone:
predator, hanging over from history.
Here, wolf and brown bear were once at home,
crystalline lynx lay in ambush for the innocent.
God wetted a finger, turned a page
and the world had a very different image.

A sky-splitting single-sloped precipice,
its lap a lemon-yellow corrie of sand,
far off a rosy panorama of mist,
curly hills in a ragged mauve cloud-band;
above, the couple stood; below, the sun-wheel stirred;
in the dawn-flames, so interdependent
they stood, afraid, at the very edge of fate;
boulders rolled from beneath their feet,
they were quarrelling, tearing their hearts,
each of them deaf before the other starts.

In the tangled thicket of their young blood
the luminous world skulks off, sinks;
shame like a rose-branch cut
the boy to the quick:
beyond entreaty, ready to throw himself down to...
His white shirt gestured against the blue,
at the shrubby scarp with its bindweed
he lurched forward, forward
growing smaller and more distant—and his frightened girl
runs after him through briars, her knee's blood is a pearl.

Tall sedges lean over the gorge
and like a gemmed porch of the depths below
an army of tiny shining shields of weeds
and a thick dark couch of green
cling round the bark of a stump that points no-
where, here their frenzy lost its rage:
they twined together, to ask why, to cry,
like the horned moon the white flash of a thigh;
a hooded boletus at their feet
fattened its spore-crammed belly, not bothering to mate.

71

The hilltop sends down
wind tasting of stone
to crochet sudden air-lace;
and the lost parasol
shivers and half lives;
in the endlessly intricate forest, in the deep maze
of its undergrowth, a breeze
lurks, but takes off at the sharp rock-fall,
pouring over that solitary wall
and across the ravine, flying light to the dale.

Zigzag mane of the thicket
wavers and swirls,
the forest depths are sighing,
a thousand tiny leaves, like birds' tails, flicker
and glint in the light like scales;
drawn up from a breeze-wakened copse
yeasty, spicy fragrances are flying;
a snapped thorn-branch stirs, drops,
catches on the soft fabric:
on the tent-like parasol the first tear is pricked.

No one is sorry—
right above it an oriole is calling,
inside it a bow-legged spider scurries
round and round the scarlet corrie
and makes off: under the metal-arched ribs
a lizard twists in search of his siesta,
he guzzles the oven-heat and like a jester
propped on both hands peeps out from the midst;
later some mice come running in and out
and the shaft has a gaudy tit perking about.

In the vault of summer skies, diamond-blue,
an ice-white lace-mist moves in a smile;
over the plain, at the foothills of heaven,
there are dark woolpacks hanging heavy
and truant cloud-lines in crumbling style;
Apollo, body stripped, striding through,
runs young, strong, and fresh,
hot oil steams on the earth's rough flesh;
in air that rocks both valley and peak,
in empty immensities—a red spot of silk.

The girl of the neglected parasol
is just as small, lost in the broad world,
a tiny insect dropped in a sea-wide flood;
        no one to talk to at all,
wrapping her own soul round her fear,
        she curls up in a curtained room,
and hears a whipped dog whining there
as if there was no misery anywhere,
no other wound to ache in earth or heaven;
or does he howl for all the pain of men?

            Hanging on the sky's arch
                at the lower bank
                    the dusk
                    is hazy.
        The first? How many before? On the lazy
        ridge no grass or insect measures it,
        neither cuckoo nor cuckoo-spit,
    the twilights turn for ever, as created.
    At the rock's edge, with forever's speed
the sleek silk vanishes into foaming shade.

Night's victory, yesterday's goodbye:
huge galley in the bay of earth and sky,
floating catafalque of dead Osiris;
scarlet embers fall into saffron high-tide,
peacock of air bends his fan from the heights,
shimmering feathers are roses and night-stocks;
an organ of gold installed in space
opens up all its pipes and lips,
pencils of light-rays spring from the rifts
and stroke the hills while darkness fills their cliffs.

            On the foamy crest of foliage
        light and shade come knotted together
            like the body's pain and pleasure.
    Fading now, from its cover, the cuckoo's message,
            and the motley unison
    of piping, chattering, chirping, splashing
            prankishness and passion.
        The evening light, that turns dreams on,
    bends through the cool slow-surging trees,
gleams in the silvery homespun of twittering beaks.

———

73

Each smallest voice is poured
delicately into the quiet;
the nightingale among thorns, like
a plucked metal string
casts a few notes into the wind,
then uncoils one ringing thread
floating and spinning,
then flicks it like a veil, languid,
then bunches it rippling, potent but light,
and it fades: into a bed carved out of quiet.

The western sky is drained
of the late dusk's arching marble veins
and the lit-up, burnt-out body of the sky
leaves a steep column of smoke,
pierced through by stars as sharp as steel:
pearl-crest of Boötes between waving trees,
Cygnus a cross drifting lazily by,
Cassiopeia with its double dagger, the rope
of the faintly glimmering Milky Way
loosely folding dead black space away.

The valley, a deep arena, rests,
crisscrossed by shadows of slashed buttresses;
in the cirque a buxom Venus dances,
approaches, spins round, offers riches,
dances naked, white as snow, touches
her feet upon the dew-drenched hills,
soft-bodied, plump, with shining curls,
the slippery form is merged in darkness,
avid monsters stare her through and through;
in a swoon she waves goodbye and the curtain snaps to.

Like rows of houses in an earthquake:
great tangle of trees at the wood's edge
stagger and shake;
a green shot flies up into the whirlwind,
a grindstone shrieking comes from rocky ledge,
the wilderness tosses and groans;
on the cloud-capped hilltop a thin
lightning burns, crackles, cracks,
then the long crisped fires streaming like flax
split above the cliff, a lion's growl at their backs.

———

The storm flickers through the twigs,
its thousand necks turn and twist,
it wrestles with the stumbling forest,
a writhing timber in its fist,
leathery roots clutch hard,
lightning tingles in the dark,
hundreds of birds crouch and start
in nests that shake them to the heart,
the burning, clammy monster rages still,
the sky, bowed low, seethes around the hill.

Torn-off leaves whirl anywhere,
roots of a gouged beech prod the air;
the parasol has been swept off the rock,
into a bramble-bush, beside a tree-trunk,
the downpour slaps its silk,
it is all smudged now, frayed, and the ribs show.
It is indifferent to its fate—as the hilltop holds
its head without complaint in thunderbolts,
and with the sky huddles low,
and fixed by sticky clouds watches the daybreak glow.

The parasol has a new home:
the secret world in fallen leaves,
cool dark earth and mouldering grove,
pallid trailers, roots in graves,
horrors endless, puffy, ropy, cold,
centipede country, maggot metropolis;
the days swing round like catapults,
casting the full sun over it, the old
weltering moon; and the parasol sprawls
like a flaking corpse, though it never lived at all.

Autumn rustles: stuffs dead leaves in it;
winter gallops: it is all snow;
the thaw sets it free again:
earth-brown, washed-out now.
A sprouting acorn pushes,
and through the slack, loose
fabric a tiny flag
thrusts the fibres back:
green, tender tassel steers to the weathervanes;
a few more years and a tree will shade the remains.

75

The parasol has changed: it has left human hands;
the girl has changed too: she is the woman of a man;
once, the red sail and the steerer ran
        lightly together, roving free,
while hosts of drunkenly foaming plum trees
tempted the wasps to stir noisily
        and deep in the girl's heart the bumble-bees
began to swarm and buzz mischievously;
since then, this wild army has been busy,
building a fortress in her woman's body.

        Both man and woman have forgotten it now,
though it was the first witness of their linked fates:
Lombard silk and red Rhine dye,
long-travelled Indian ivory,
Pittsburgh iron, Brazilian wood, how
        many handcarts have trundled its parts,
        they have gone by rail, they have gone in boats:
a world to make it! son of a thousand hands!
yet no curio: old-world frippery;
lost: no joy in that, yet no great misery.

Branching veins draw it into the dark,
        light-unvisited mud weighs it down,
it is mere rags, dying in dribs and drabs,
it has stopped serving exotic demands
and like a bird escaping its cage-door
        takes up its great home:
the dissolving soil, the swirl of space, the rays
draw it all ways, confused, astray,
old shoreless floods map its new phase:
this is creation's first emergent day.

        Neither sun, moon, nor watch
        can measure creation's second and third days:
        the father of vegetation keeps his watch
over it, clod-head, Saturn, dark face
with grey eyebrows hanging to his chin.
        Pulsing life-fluid filters in:
powdered cloth, rotten wood, rusted iron
dissolve and disappear in tangle and thorn,
and slowly sucked by each capillary vein
it seethes alive again in the humming vortex of green.

———

Its handle is visible through the leaf-mould.
A brown moth settles there, perches awhile.
      By midnight it has laid
hundreds of eggs, a mass of tiny balls
placed in smooth strips, finely embroidered.
And like a biblical ancestress
she opens her wings, floats victorious,
queen fulfilled in happiness,
      not caring that dawn brings death:
God in the sky drew up my trembling crest!

The parasol no longer exists: bit by bit
      it set off into the open world,
      all changed, part after part;
even the eyes of Argus might find no trace,
      swivelling across the light,
      sliding down to the shade;
      only a single feeble fibre remains,
      poised on the top of a bramble-prickle,
      it is mere fluff, next to invisible;
flies up from the thorn-prick, jumps into the saddle

of a storm! Lily-thin air-pockets toss it on,
      the mountains shift below
in stampede, buffalo trampling buffalo;
fog-blanket opens on dark forest paths,
brooks twinkling down in the shy straths,
sharp drop of the crag wall, a mine,
toy trains of tubs moving along the rails,
scattered homesteads, a town with its smoke-trails,
and overhead, the great bleak acres of silence
and below, the hill from which the tuft went flying.

Upwards, still higher up it floats:
the moon hangs close like a white fruit,
the earth is a round, tilted, blotchy shroud
      framed by blackness and void.
      Bathed in airy juices,
the fluff swings heavy like a full leather bottle,
      descends to the ground, settles:
      on a green plain, in drizzly mists,
it hovers lightly among the acacias
and probes a calf's ear as its resting-place.

A thunderstorm crashes, carries it off,
flies with it raggedly over moor and bog,
like a spool it turns, winding the fog,
        and when it is all spun onto a distaff:
low blue sea and high blue sky are combers,
        two sun discs gaze at each other
        and between the two blue shells
                a tiny sail
                sways, tranquil,
uncaring whether it sways in air or swell.

The vapour-tulip throws back its head,
a glass-green other-worldly meadow glistens,
at the horizon a purple thorn gathers;
darkness surrounds the far-off island;
a little ray like a woman's glance flickers,
vanishes caressing the lover, glitters
as it flutters onto its drowsy son,
while a smile dawns eternity on man,
        its arches bend and march on their way
between watery shores, Theatrum Gloriae Dei.

* * *

The red silk parasol was my song,
        sung for my only one;
this true love is the clearest spring,
        I have smoothed its mirror with my breath,
I have seen the two of us, the secret is known:
        we shall moulder into one after death.
Now I expend my life exultantly
like the oriole in the tree:
        till it falls down on the old forest floor,
singing with such full throat its heart must burst and soar.

[1953]   *Edwin Morgan*

Le Journal

a mare ran into the yard
a cedar caught her sight
virginal phenomena paired
"its image is my spirited spirit"

O to sing in Horsish
bitted and bridled by the Muse
the saddle receiving Orpheus
ode psalm hymn in my jaws

Chung-kuo Hellas France Mizraim
would marvel at my hoofs of porcelain
my white lamp my socks prim
beyond the lasts of our understanding

a spherical breviary would come
up gratis sogar
I'd need no honorarium
only heavenly fire

I'd lift into the light of the sun
I'd fall into the dew of the moon
with sweet fruit pouring in
the hieroglyphics of my skeleton

anthropoid heaven-dwellers by the score
would be houyhnhnmized in my horsehood
and Xenophon's belief be proved
if I sang to my horsely score

the apehead is an evil pitcher
heavenly sparks prance there
and sink back to cinders in matter
as soon as they are music and picture

on the plain the bacchanalia
on the peaks King Zeus in the abyss
Aphrodite Pelagia
coral-reef in purple darkness

Helen's brothers in the skies
far flame no spit can sting
your groin-spasm in heavenly fires
you've as much domestique orang

your hand creates no more
than a fold on Diotima's robe
and she smooths it on her breast
to shine where it was pressed

thinking about the authority
of Attica of Italia
a stoa of babblers actually
serenade for Garufalia

one morning I get up early
look stomachly footly handly
my loving Garufalia
is in love with Garufalia

I gaze at you O Garufalia
mirror-wall of my being
I sniff my own snout finally
self reconciles everything

but lifelike side by side
shepherd shouts sheep graze
man and worm forage
on woman horse and other gods

orang komm her look around
no mango palm liana sandalwood
your country dreams in other images
concrete bulks steel stretches

on the shore of the city's man-din
the field's girl-body lies
with stripped hills the victim
of shuddering technologies

Danube gets the gull's droppings
the swallows shit on the porches
a Hittite king goes jigging
under Lajos Kossuth's portrait

balsam for all the inhabitants
to make the limb sweet as a violet
mummies shut in mastabas
you're a Hittite don't deny it

the Hittite the Hittite
a strange race is the Hittite
it's believed by every Hittite
everybody else is Hittite

an odd bird is the gull
it's believed by every gull
that whenever he meets a gull
it is never really a gull

let your dreams revolve your potential
it grows light over the city
the dustman starts up early
his nag no Pegasus after all

in the fading whirlpool of stars
his dagger-point stabs flying paper
while Debrecen wakens on the shores
of the Ganges where palm trees waver

Sárika goes in her sarong
by the Déri Museum for a stroll
musk-smells drift along
by the six-footed Golden Bull

endless dreams of the plains
painted on mirage-soft seas
Aurengzebe's mosque raised
above Hindu temple-cornices

waves from Debrecen's Great Wood
flood a sleek barber's shop
snails octopuses are whirled up
mirrors lose their drowsy mood

attentive assistants in white
stand in water to their brows
customers in the muddy pit
foam infusoria on their scowls

patch on patch the sea grows
Golgotha is drenched Csokonai
hangs on a giant cross
Tóth and Gulyás by his side*

oh I need no foolscap to write
for if I should shed my skin
the same dumb witness would rise
from the hieroglyphics of my skeleton

what I don't know let me say
what I do know let me hide
and when tomorrow flies and I stay
I am asked and my skeleton replies

what I don't think let me declare
and what I do think let me conceal
shut up the truth the fake is shrill
the rest must be clawed from its lair

in chinks between lines of verse
angels and prophets cluster
the paper's whitest space
worth more than any letter

* Csokonai, Tóth, Gulyás:
Hungarian poets born in Debrecen

creation never bettered a stroll
blessed trackless periplum
but the pyramid's no joke at all
clinging to each minute-long millennium

the sewer clogs you with weed
to keep you here in the world
Homo Esothericus and your fellows
droves of Homo Bestialis

the sisterhood of Narcissa
recommend a solitary love-in
and the goat-breeders' synod
adopts the puny faun

Hellene eye and Hebrew sight
have their lines crossed in such a state
that hell-egg and heaven-fruit
make pining-apple omelette

orang geh weg give no sign
you are a useless oracle
all this is natural miracle
says Franz Kafka the divine

already both sides of our moustache
hold little bubbles in a net
and there is a rout of goldfish
from jaws now wide and wet

the whole aquarium wakes
to a throbbing panicky stir
the old cupboard shakes
and even the thermometer

but the dingy family faces
look blankly down from the walls
winking no come-ye-alls
either to us or the fishes

marvel rather at the charger
it knows indescribable things
its smile in its soul is larger
than any its lips could bring

its harness and saddle are alien
yet it bears them if laid on
all it shuns is the muddy fountain
and the fallow field is its domain

what it accomplishes the many tasks
are not for it to meditate
by the time it has its questions asked
its hide squeaks on our feet.

[1953]   *Edwin Morgan*

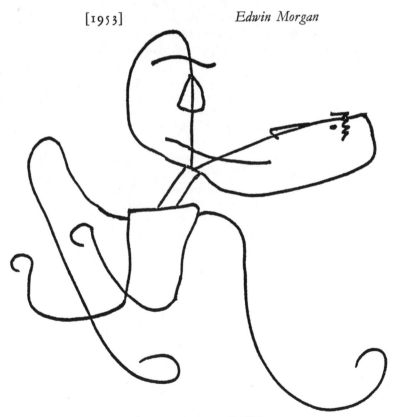

SOMEONE DOUBTING HIMSELF

Moon and Farmstead

full   moon   slip   swim
wind   fog   foam   chord   hum
the   house   empty

rampant
thorn   fence
eye   blaze

moon   swim   flame
grass   chord   twang
cloud   fling

the   house   empty
door   window
fly   up

chimney   run
fog   swirl
full   moon   circle

the   house   empty

[1954]   *Edwin Morgan*

Monkeyland

Oh for far-off monkeyland,
ripe monkeybread on baobabs,
and the wind strums out monkeytunes
from monkeywindow monkeybars.

Monkeyheroes rise and fight
in monkeyfield and monkeysquare,
and monkeysanatoriums
have monkeypatients crying there.

Monkeygirl monkeytaught
masters monkeyalphabet,
evil monkey pounds his thrawn
feet in monkeyprison yet.

Monkeymill is nearly made,
miles of monkeymayonnaise,
winningly unwinnable
winning monkeymind wins praise.

Monkeyking on monkeypole
harangues the crowd in monkeytongue,
monkeyheaven comes to some,
monkeyhell for those undone.

Macaque, gorilla, chimpanzee,
baboon, orangutan, each beast
reads his monkeynewssheet at
the end of each twilight repast.

With monkeysupper memories
the monkeyouthouse rumbles, hums,
monkeyswaddies start to march,
right turn, left turn, shoulder arms—

monkeymilitary fright
reflected in each monkeyface,
with monkeygun in monkeyfist
the monkeys' world the world we face.

[1955]   *Edwin Morgan*

EL DORADO

from *Orpheus*

ORPHEUS KILLED

I lie in a cold shaded courtyard, I am dead.
They sob over my body, so many women, men.
Grief rolls from the drum and I start dancing. Who
killed me, why?

      I drift round the market, in palaces,
in taverns, among the flute-players, till in drink
I can say to the drunk: Look at me, I am
your hearts: engaged to death for the sake
of beggars and the blind.

        Stone I am and metal I am
on a slave's cross. The corpse is staring wide-eyed,
grief rolls from the drum and I dance. I am everything
and I am nothing: oh, look at me. I am everyone
and I am no one: stone and metal, many shapes,
on a slave's cross. Why did the priests kill me?
Did I slight their temple?

        Dismembered I lie in the wasteland,
what urn is there for my white dust? Why
did the women tear me? Do they want my dead love?

Wolves of the famished earth prowl all round me,
decay rains rolling down and I start dancing.
Cain I am and saint I am: kneel at my feet.
Leper I am and clean I am: touch me. Body
moves, weak joints crack, cold tears trickle, he
sweats, sweats. Mindless I am and wise I am,

ask no questions, understand in silence. Dead I am
and alive I am, a dumb face, I. A wax-face
sacrifice turns skyward, ringed by staring horror, grief
rolls from the drum and I dance.

       No asking back the body stretched on the cross.
I lie harvested in the wasteland,
no asking back the grain laid up in barns.
Death's drum rolls, I whirl in the dance for ever,
the song flooding the valley refreshed by my blood,
my secret endless life entangled in the groves of death.

[1955]   *Edwin Morgan*

ALL IS BROKEN AND ALL OBSERVES

Queen Tatavane

O my winged ancestors!
Green branch and dry twig you gave me
for my two empires, to plant one and to lash one.
I am small as a weasel, pure as the eastern Moon,
light-ankled as a gazelle, but not poised for flight—
my heart lies open to you, to every silent suggestion.

The Elephantstar took my fifteenth year,
the Dragonstar brought this, the sixteenth.
I am allowed three husbands by ancestral decree
and seven lovers beneath the holy jasmine-leaves.

Not for me to escape with girl-friends to the fields,
for happy laughter, goats to milk, fresh milk to drink,
instead I sit on the throne in your light, year after year,
an ebony idol with the world's weight on my neck.

Negro caravans, Arab ships are my traffic and merchandise,
I pay well, though I see most as polecats and monkeys,
but even the sky rains on unchosen ground, seeds burst unchosen.
I survey the naked hosts lost in their prison,
all of them I love as if they were my children,
punishing them with the rod and if need be by the sword,
and though my heart should bleed my looks are frozen.

Wake up, my fathers and mothers! Leave the ash-filled urn,
help me while the mists crawl;
your dark little daughter pleads with you as the last queen,
waiting among the garlands of the cedar-hall.

My seat among stone lions, the man's throne empty at my side,
my brow is glowing ruby-wreathed like the dawn-clouds,
my purple-tinted fingers, my drowsy almond eyes
shine like a god's as they strike down and raise;
what you found sweet and bitter I come to, I taste.

Orange veils on my shoulders, fireflower wreaths on my dark hair,
the reedpipe cries, the eunuchs drone, the altar's set.
Come Bulak-Amba my starry bull-browed ancestor!
Come Aure-Ange my lovely holy milk-rich ancestress!

Mango, areca, piled on the altar,
the year's brimming rice, brown coconut, white copra,
all round, red flower thrown on red flower,
sweet sandalwood fumes float up into the air.

Great man-spirit with no name: eat!
Great woman-spirit with no name: eat!
Huge emptiness in the silence behind the drumbeat: eat!

I call you, my father over the foam,
my old begetter, Batan-Kenam,
you are coming in your sun-chariot, four-elephant-drawn,
through the head-waving rattlesnakes of five cosmic storms,
my soldier, ageless, coral-garlanded,
blue-shirted arms,
lance of sky's shark-bone, turtle shield,
cut-off locks of the seven dancer-stars shimmer at your belt,
your elephants lumber and stamp, tiger-herds are felled,
and you rest on your elbow at the world's end in the lee of the
                                    loud blue mountain—
I salute you my glittering visitor, my far-off father!

I am wrapped in my veil, I am hidden,
the welcoming hostess is timid,
I hand out half-peeled oranges on a gold dish:
look at me here, I am your own flesh,
you know I am supple and clawed like a forest cat,
you pause if you see my dark green shining eyes,
my white-hot teeth-embers,
behind, my skeleton is lace-fine, a dragonfly:
see your one-day-old woman! one smile is all she would wish!

I summon you Aruvatene, my mother!
I call you. I am your daughter. Do you love her?
Your little one, will you be her protector?
Look, Nightqueen, at your tiny drop of dew:
the sparkling skin, the swelling breast!
You thick-starred heavenly palm tree, I dance for you.
Blow the pipe, roll the drum,
my dance-wind skims about you, let it come!
my silver ankle-jangle chatters—from you it came!
my orange shawl flies out—you gave it my name!

But if your beautiful face goes ashy as mist
I give you my blood to drink from your ancient chalice,
turn back, I leave you in peace,
eat, drink in silence.

Come too, Andede, good grandmother,
you are as old as the wind
that snuffles in the oven-cinders.
I shall never be so old,
fugitive with blowing flowers.

Andede, good grandmother,
you are as wrinkled as the stone
that snaps off from the mountain.
I shall never be so wrinkled,
I am the rock-escaping fountain.

Andede, good grandmother,
you smile like a yellow desert place
grinding its bones, toothless sand-cascades
skirting the cosmic border.
That is not my smile,
I am the lady of two empires,
sword and bread on my lap together
under the trickle of my tears.

Andede, good grandmother,
you champ and smack like the green dragon
that swallows up the wildest moor.
But I can never be satisfied,
two nations fight to eat from my hand
and bread forever lusts after sword.

———

Andede, good grandmother,
perpetually decaying, never destroyed,
you are puny but sinewy like a root in the earth,
I am the mother of everybody,
I would take them all on my lap,
I would let them all eat and sup,
but when I even raise my hand, I die.

Great man-spirit with no name: eat!
Great woman-spirit with no name: eat!
Huge emptiness in the silence behind the drumbeat: eat!

Come forward, now, great, ancient, unforgotten,
every sky-dome-breasted queen,
every lightning-dashing king!
I know that your good
is our only food,
but if misery surges again,
here I am—my blame alone,
I your shadow, your orphan,
prostrate under your cane,
beg for that bastinadoing!

For heaven's sake help me then!
Oh I am the virgin peahen
who instead of living eggs
found redhot stones between her legs
and with anxious wings spread wide
broods to hatch a void.
Pain of two nations is fire under me,
who will ever hatch the happiness of the world?

[1956]   *Edwin Morgan*

Ars Poetica

Memory cannot make your song everlasting.
Glory is not to be hoped from the evanescences:
how could it glorify you, when its glitterings are not essences?
Your song may flaunt a few embers from eternal things
while those who face them take fire as a minute passes.

Sages suggest: only individuals are in their senses.
All right; but to get more, be more than individual:
slip off your great-poet status, your lumbering galoshes,
serve genius, give it your human decencies
which are point and infinity: neither big nor small.

Catch the hot words that shine in the soul's estuaries:
they feed and sustain countless earth-centuries
and only migrate into your transient song,
their destiny is eternity as your destiny is,
they are friends who hug you and hasten soaring on.

[1956]   *Edwin Morgan*

In Memoriam Gyula Juhász*

Let the beasts whine at your grave my father
whine at your grave
let the beasts whine
between the byre and the blade
between the slaughterhouse and dunghill
between the clank of the chain and desolation
my mother as Hamlet said
let the old hunchbacked women whine
between the hospital and the glad rags
between the asylum and the lily-of-the-valley
between the cemetery and the frippery
and the wretches with buried ulcers
between stately doctors and strapping priests
all those paralysed by deferred release
on the far side of hope on the near side of confrontation

Let butterflies twist above the stream
Ophelia who drowned before we were born
the roseless thorn is yours
the profitless pain
the lacklustre ghost in a mourning frame
the falling on knees face in the mud
the humiliation boundless and endless
the dead body without a cross
the unredeemed sacrifice
the hopelessness that is for ever hopelessness

Let rabid dogs howl at your grave
let hollow phantoms hoot
my starry brother my bearded bride
the good is only a moment's presentiment
evil is not eternal malice
in the meantime blood flows
lacerated life cannot die
death is deathless liberty

[1957]   *Edwin Morgan*

* Hungarian poet, 1883–1937.

Terra Sigillata

EPIGRAMS OF AN ANCIENT POET

I

Useless interrogation: I know nothing. An old man fallen asleep,
I wake as a baby, and you can read your learning from my
wide blue eyes; I only glimpse it in recidivist streams.

2

A red-figered child pats grey cakes at the seaside,
I ask for one, he says no, not even for a real cake, no.
Well now, old prophets, what do you want from me? the twenty-four
sky prisms, when I look blind into hearts and read them.

3

If you want your fortune, I'll reel off your identity, your expectations,
but I'm deaf to my own words—no plundering secrets.

4

"You say you're God's offspring: why do you scrape along like
                                                    paupers?"
"Even Zeus himself, when he takes human steps on earth,
begs bread and water, parched, starved as a tramp."

5

The Dazzling is always coming to earth to beg for mud,
while his palace in heaven, stiff with gold, sighs for his return.

6

The bowed-down carrier looks up: there he stands at the centre
                                                    of the earth!
It is above his head that the sky's vault goes highest.

7

Beautiful the lonely pine, beautiful the bee-wreathed rose,
beautiful the white funeral, most beautiful through all—their union.

8

The treasures of a tree! Leaves, flowers, fruits.
How freely it gives them, clinging to the elements alone.

9

The forest has modesty, the wolf hides his death in the shadows,
but a bought mourner will shrill without shame at a stranger's burial.

10

The swindler doesn't slip up with his bogus balance-sheets when
his heart is firm,
but when bursting out crying and taking pity on the innocent.

11

Crime has majesty, virtue is holy; but what is the troubled heart
worth?
There, crime is raving drunk and virtue is a jailer.

12

The moment I slice the cocoon of my fate: my skull is the sky-dome
fate-shuttling stars scuttle across its arch.

[1958]   *Edwin Morgan*

Mountain Landscape

Valley brook
birdsong squabble.

High quiet
home of god-faced
rocks hanging.

And higher, Nemo's song,
hilltop grindstone-squeal:
ice cracks smart.

[1959]   *Edwin Morgan*

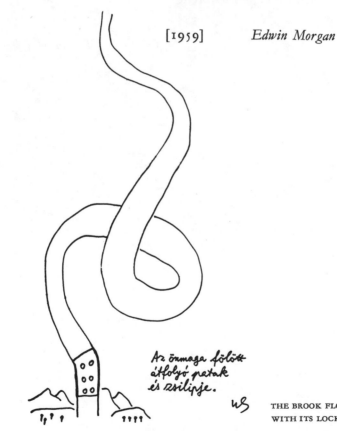

Az önmaga fölött
átfolyó patak
és zsilipje.   wz

THE BROOK FLOWING OVER ITSELF
WITH ITS LOCK

Wallpaper and Shadows

grape vine tendril bunch grape vine tendril bunch grape vine tendril b
ne tendril bunch grape vine tendril bunch grape vine tendril bunch gra
nch grape vine tendril bunch grape vine tendril bunch grape vine tend
    qip   qip   qip   qip   qip   qip
     qip qip   qip qip   qip qip
       qip   qip   qip
   vintage waits   vintage waits   vintage waits
basket grows on barrow basket grows on barrow basket grows on barr
   to the hill   to the hill   to the hill
     qip   qip   qip
   qip qip   qip qip   qip qip
qip   qip   qip   qip   qip   qip
vine tendril bunch grape vine tendril bunch grape vine tendril bunch g
ne tendril bunch grape vine tend SUDDENLY THERE ARE TWO TWILIGHTS
il bunch grape vine tendril bunch grape vine BOTH DONE ONLY IN PAINTS
   qip   qip   qip   THE REAL ONE IS THE THIRD
    qip qip   qip   LIKE A BEGGAR STANDS OUTSIDE
     qip   qip   qip

[1963]   *Edwin Morgan*

Rayflower

Rayflower
about the head
so flickery
then fled

Above the shoulders
below the chin
a lonely night-light
is carried in

In front of the chest
lace-foam flying
already the fire there
fading dying

In the swelling
of the belly
a shadow spreads
enormously

In a dark sea
no foot lingers
fearing to leave
the lucifer fingers

[1959]   *Edwin Morgan*

Illusionists and Their Victims

Those I thought dreamily superior to life—the
earthly counterparts of fairies and other rainbow-
hued delusions—were on the one hand women; and on
the other the *castrati* of old, wine-pouring handsome
boys, circus athletes, comedians, lute- and flute-
players, the priests, the augurs, the magicians.

I thought they drank with their victims to make them
tipsy, while remaining murderously sober themselves—
and the only one blinded by intoxication was a Man.

They dissolve desire to draw its knot the tighter,
while they are quite without desire themselves—
and the only one who feels yearning is a Man.

With them even death is a deception: they can smooth
the eye like marble to bring despair to a climax,
while they themselves watch for the quivering nothing
from the nothingness beyond—and the only one who
dies, whether bravely or wretchedly, is a Man.

A Man who heroically and madly bares his chest, while
the others just stoke his fever, stash his silver,
and laugh up their cuffs.

It is not so. I have seen the drunken waiter, the pub
musician sobbing in the ditch, the abandoned actress
and credulous *credo*-ing priest. Nor is this girl
some soporific bit of fluff any more, she comes from
work on the leaden feet of a log-rolling elephant,
and drinks her glass of self-deception, just like a Man.

Was I then the last of the confidence men whom women
saw as helpless, men saw as mad, the last of those
who could look back with the glance of a child and yet
be sober as a knife inside?

Was I then a lodging for the last whore of all, the
one who robs and is not robbed because from her bun
to her bum she's simply a bubble?

Was I then the ultimate hermaphrodite whose birth as
male was mere pretence, who when his part was ended
carefully closed the door?

Pah, there's nothing final. In the dry bed of a river,
in another season, the flood streams.

We, women and *castrati* alike, should be silent.
Satisfied to come and go through the portals of life
and death, accomplices in the great delusion.

We seem to be a riddle, though the real riddle's the
man with the dropping burden, the bag of treasures,
the illusory fantasy in his heart; the one with
stubborn ideas which he projects on to us, in which
supposed act of compassion he breathes freely a
moment and thinks he has lost his solitude.

For thousands of years we've been in the habit of
marvelling at his intelligence, opening our eyes in
wonder—and why not, when clad in armour he flings
treasure at us, and sets out afterwards with his
tools, his dagger, with grevious pain, to attain
something in order to lose it.

But the glory—the glory of the fight and of stepping
blindly into death—is Man's.

Unknowing he marries that nest of desire, the Mother;
but knowing he atones for it. Bisexual Tiresias,
surrender to Oedipus, the Man!

[1959]   *Hugh Maxton*

A Session of the World Congress

A white-hot glow as every brain
glitters in diagonal section,
a chief from Papua chairs the session,
face to face with Britain's queen,

a princess of Upepe's crown
chews her quid with mobile lips
while the French ambassador keeps
his face from being a spittoon,

a Bazongan pair swing from the lights
but since they know decorum's steps,
love scatters its obliquer drops

in rainbow arcs of mays and mights:
one more year of shuffling chips,
and they'll have an agenda, perhaps.

[1959]   *Edwin Morgan*

THE THREE-ARMED ONE

Difficult Hour

Time for black prophecies is over: the Winter of History
is whistling around us.

Man, with suicidal power in his limbs, poison in his blood,
craziness in his head like a mad dog: nobody can see his
destiny.

If he wants to scarify people to the bone with his new
instruments of devastation: his only attainments are loss
of the wheel and of fire, forgetfulness of speech, life on all
fours.

But let him extricate himself: let him give up his myriad
maggot-teeming acts of idiot self-will, his termite provision-
activities for the outer world: first let him measure and order
the inner world.

Familiar and ordered inner worlds outgrow individual
greed, learn to rub along with one another, even to be in
harmony with their outer world.

This is the only practicable way. Up till now, the blood-
stained currents of history may have moved with beauty
and grandeur but moved to a common death, or worse,
narrowed their streams to the further agony of a relentless
dehumanization.

But today some cradle rocks a fire-baby bringing divine
gifts such as we hardly saw in our dreams.

And just as in bygone days they laid open the secret
strength of the material world: they will begin now to lay
open the powers of the bodiless inner world.

In the hands of these children the lamp of reason does not
dictate, but serve: shining through subconscious life-forces
and supraconscious spirit-forces alike, illuminating them
and setting them to work in turn.

It was always others man conquered in the past; but—
oh tremulous hope!—in the future he conquers himself,
and fate subdues itself before him, and the stars.

[1960]   *Edwin Morgan*

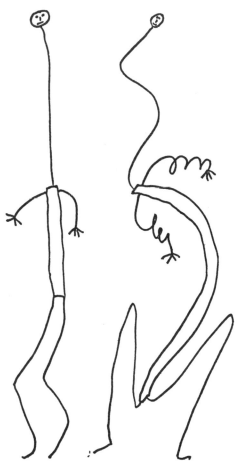

PROPOSITION

In the Window-Square

In the window-square
a star clots
on black sky
dull light forms a minute
the trees surge darkly
distant sea sings in leaves
the wind butts the curtain with its forehead
outside your tight-shut minutes
your star tears you away
the infinite flows and foams through the garden
but in this room space is concentrated
drowns in angle and bay
on red slopes of the armchair
stretches transparently
on the tendril-blue neck of the ewer
flies up to stay
your ring on the table
inextinguishable candle
night slaps the island
hear the sea lapping
things in their deaf shells
clotting in the window-frame
grief hangs over a deep
you picture-book of the universe
in full-lighted age-old existence
shut now at a touch
but my eye runs over the cover
as this star wanders
with its light-year rays
with its blank shoreless gaze

[1961]   *Edwin Morgan*

The Double I

Out of the globe of an unfamiliar lamp
I am unfolded, beaming,
on a lengthening shadow stepping
from the more and more distant country
and voices that escape,
from sweat, through crosses I have sold,
the hundred cindered butterfly antennae,
a thousand bloody fingernails that crimp
into a garland, beneath me, deeply holed,
the other's agitated thump:

"Wait—I am here as well, I am your slime!
I am noosed in the seaweed of dark.
My eyes from seven miles can be seen to look,
I know the trouble in their gleam,
each hue finds its reflection there;
like those of a crack hunting hound,
at the slightest sound my sharp ears prick;
replete yourself, you leave me here to suffer,
among the broken bottles I am thirsty,
yet in your bosom's grieved outpouring drowned.

"You do not know the torrent which you pour
on me, which you have poured with such profusion;
perhaps a mist drop is enough to please you;
the price-boards which they score
in black at markets are my own
and show the ephemeral for sale,
so that I topple, lose myself and dive
in the flash of a shooting star;
eternal death, I cannot bear
this barren vault I beg you to remove!"

I travel on, don't hear this sad insistence,
and from the lost horizon I look back;
a tower obscured within a thick
ash-cloud is guardian of the distance;
I do not know what is to come,
and all my power to think is numb;
I would not mind the earth swallowing up
that other one the hole entombs;
he'll be the only listener to the music
till the Last Judgement comes.

[1962]   *Alan Dixon*

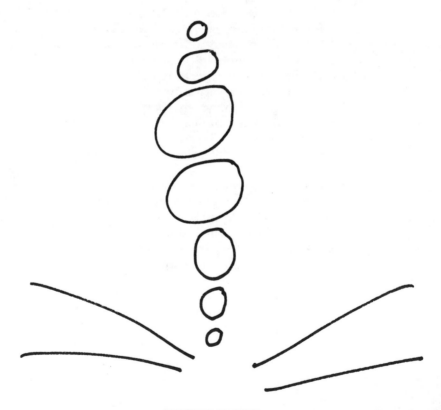

EXPLOSION OR MUSIC

Internus

GROWING OLD

My brain's gutterings unwind,
its light—that poverty of mind—
keeps drawing in its radius,
keeps glowing in still dimmer space;
with God's help, I shall hardly see
how far off the cell-wall may be.

SELF-PORTRAIT WITH DOG

The man I was is dying, his gasps are faint:
the heart is like a stone that stops the throat.
The life-spark, to get back its breath, leaps out
at long last from the miserable body
into a dog, to find tranquillity.
I lay my head down on my master's foot.
I don't feel his pain, I don't remember. I don't.

DISSOLVING PRESENCE

It's not my self that interests me,
only that my death, so certain,
saves me from unwanted clowning,
though a tramped-on worm can hurt me.
Is dying going into nothing?
No more despair, no more desire.
But after-life may be no plaything?
I can endure from fire to fire.
Life and death don't interest me,
I only need that harmony
which matter cannot even bear
or reason take into its sphere.

DOUBLE-FACED

My self: though this perpetual guest
is hardly boring company,
he's a tick to bite my privacy,
without him I'd have quiet and rest.
Because he's attentive to my demon
and shapes its early hints in words
I put up with his earthy being
till evening ends, not afterwards.

OUT OF THE INNER INFINITY

From inward infinities I still look out
now and again, seeing through my face
clouds or the winking lights of stars in space.
My eyesight fails, that leaves me like the rest,
the outside world has shut my gates, I'm left
where there is no earth left, but only sky;
and no event, no grace and no surprise,
no surface, nothing seen, no nebulas,
only reality at peace and luminous,
boundless and measureless and nameless,
a love that's still desireless and still changeless.

The panic world is baffled at my gate:
"Madman! Egotist! Traitor!" its words beat.
But wait: I have a bakehouse in my head,
you'll feed someday on this still uncooled bread.

THE MUDDY DRINK IS GOING DOWN
AND THE BOTTOM OF THE GLASS
SHOWS THROUGH

After death shall I still exist?
No handcuffs then upon my wrist,
I have dissolved identity,
why wish it in eternity?
Being or non-being: nakedness
suits undying presences.

I never thought it could be so:
my body gasps for its last breath,
yet still and easy is my soul.
My life is wantless and unwanted,
a beggar going on undaunted,
even by my death unhaunted,
with losses and with gains untaunted.
Fate is too kind! I had best not
die this way, like a dying god,
a smiling victory well flaunted;
I should be pulled up by the root
with a cowardly last shout
and get the real end of a man,
not judged for what I solely am.

NOCTURNE

Bored with my being, unutterably,
boxed in male bones perpetually,
I'm given no rest from his presence,
he and I are old bed-fellows,
I can feel his warmth, his sweat,
from his hair-roots to his feet,
feel the twistings of his bowels,
his man's-stump and his milkless nipples,
the wheezing of his lung-bellows,
his heart-beats on uneasy pedals,
his gnawing and his stabbing pains,
his lusts that break the lagging reins,
his times of hunger and of thirst,
his filled-and-emptied bag of dust,
and what he feels and thinks within
I feel and think, unmoved, with him.
In beastly body-warmth I lie
stuck to a drumming rancid sty.
His daytime braying makes me sick
like his dead snoring, I can't stick
his senses' narrow window-glass,
the wooden O of his mind, a mass
of memories, symbols parroted
hand in hand and madly led.

I'm sick of dandling, pampering him,
of wiping the tarry rump of him,
of taking in his hungry cares,
of making his head utter prayers;
I've been his patient unpaid slave,
caring nothing for what I gave.
Not executioner, but guard,
I hold him close, but killing's barred:
he will die someday just the same,
die in peace or die in pain.
Each cell and seed he has, in its fervour
would go on fucking and gorging for ever,
and the pitiful keen-kindled mind
for ever have new knowledge to find,
but clenched in vice of flesh, I stiffen
in cramps of an enclosing coffin.
His life and stir are my own death,
and I fly on his final breath
into the love of God, fly back
till I'm a stitch in nothing's sack
and need no longer share my soul
or body with my self at all,
being unbounded plenitude,
the latency not understood
who taking all things into him
pours his wealth from a stintless brim.

[1963]   *Edwin Morgan*

The Secret Country

One day we'll jump on a floating log, E Daj the distant is
waiting for us,
we'll float on the log, wing-locked butterflies,
dance gently downwards through the traveller's-joy
beneath the sea, no one aware of us.

Below earth and sea there is a black lake,
motionless and mirror-sharp,
no one knows its chasms:
E Daj the distant is waiting for us,
one day we'll jump on a floating log, plunge in.

The old men say:
As long as we live,
everything we see
hangs in that mirror in the lake,
our faces, our figures
figured facing down.
The palms, the lianas, the foxes, the stars
all hang there in the mirror of the lake.

Short-lived the butterfly, but it visits the old farmhouse,
puttering about it with its whispering
wings, we hear them whispering,
we run, run into the house.
We don't speak to it, we don't speak to shadows.
It knocks at the door, knocks and knocks, breaks off, goes
back home,
E Daj the distant is waiting for us.

The old men say:
Our faces and figures are reflected in the black lake,
no one sees its depths:
whatever is, was once in them,
whatever was once in them, falls back there,
and this is the eternal return.

The man throws his spear, bends his bow,
the woman scrapes a hole for the fire,
all look for handholds, build huts:
and this is how we live, hanging head down in the mirror
                                        of the lake,
one day we'll jump on a floating log, plunge in.
We can't see what lies below. E Daj the distant is
                                        waiting for us.

[1963]   *Edwin Morgan*

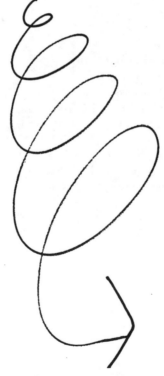

RUSHING IN AND RECOILING

Coolie

Coolie cane chop.
Coolie go
     go
        only softly-softly
   Rickshaw
   Car
   Dragon-carriage
Coolie pull rickshaw.
Coolie pull car.
Coolie pull dragon-carriage
         only softly-softly
Coolie go foot.
Coolie beard white.
Coolie sleepy.
Coolie hungry.
Coolie old.
Coolie bean poppyseed little child
big wicked man beat little Coolie
         only softly-softly
   Rickshaw
   Car
   Dragon-carriage
Who pull rickshaw?
Who pull car?
Who pull dragon-carriage?
Suppose Coolie dead.
Coolie dead.
Coolie no-o-o-t know dead!
Coolie immortal.
      only softly-softly

[1931, 1967]   *Edwin Morgan*

Saturn Declining

In memory of T. S. Eliot

They took my flock away. Should I care? I have nothing to do now,
no responsibility; easy an old man's life at the poorhouse.
Firstly they chased the priest, that antlered rambler,
off his springboard, from which he took to the sky daily—fool!—
and appointed more clever priests; then deposed the king, the defender
undefended, and welcomed the sabre-rattling kings; then the sage,
saying, We have enough scholars as it is; lastly the poet:
What is he counting his fingers for anyway, prattling? Singers,
styled to requirement, flock in his place as a consequence.

So I stand, face turned to the wall, with broken crook.
My flock jostles at the through: how many bright, brand new
splendid things are swimming in it! nose at nose, pushed nose nosing
away—should I care? It's not my vocation any more;
they stick teeth in me if I look; what will happen to the enormous
progeny, the scraped womb, ravenous,
stupefied, quickening, and the murderous rays,
the explosive left at the doorway—
                              As it is when a train
rushes towards the deep with no shore on the other side—
should I care?—maybe they'll stop it at any moment;
there could be tracks to carry it over the chasm, perhaps I am blind;
perhaps, at the edge of the abyss, it will open its wings, and fly;
they know. I do not. Their problem, if they do not.
All the same to me now: my shepherd's crook broken,
so easy to lie about in the straw, resting
from centuries of toil. They can't see, their heads in the trough;
I only see their rumps and flapping ears.

[1967]
Alan Dixon

The Seventh Garden

Never another garden where the clock
has stopped among the lilies, without hands.
      Time is counted there
no more than shade and starlight hemmed by leaves.
Does he to whom the Angel beckons linger
      still, revisiting
that place of sun whose diary is told
with a bell of stone, oblivion
turning on the marble of the columns?

Even turning face to face, they stand
with backs to us, all whispering afar
      in the garden. Days
to come are left behind if, fallible
and pale, they dare not brave the sun's bright blade.
      Tomorrows will return
if our kerchief should be left in them,
caught on the railings of the copper day
shredded gladly by the spikes of sun.

Drowsy the garden, yet pure sorrow's here,
though who'd not weep for happiness if tears
      could well from dew-washed statues
such as we are... How can I help desiring
you who scorched me? Figure slim as flame,
      lead me from this place
of silence, let me follow after, clutching
at your green sparks, beloved, like an infant
at a loose thread on a mother's dress!

[1967]   *Daniel Hoffman*

Variations on the Themes of Little Boys

1

When I'm six I'll marry Ibby
And drive a big Mercedes—Ibby
Won't get in it—she can't come
Cause she'll have to stay at home

2

CHARLIE IS A FOOL
JONIE IS A FOOL
    NOT ME—IM REEL COOL
    I got brains evry place—
    LOOKIT—even up my ass

3

    Squads, right
    Squads, left
I lead the squad—Hup! Ha!
We're going to bury my Grandma!

4

Watch my Daddy build a house:
First the chimney puffing smoke
Next beneath it comes the roof
Then the windows front and back
Can't see through them they're so black
But you can see through the walls
Because they are not there at all
Now the walls are on their way
And one by one the rooms around
When the house gets to the ground
My Daddy cries, "Hip, Hip, Hooray!"

5

Tommy, running through the yard,
Catches Suzy, beats her hard—
Out of her beats the bejesus—
Then cuts her up in little pieces,
Strings her innards heart and liver
From one fence over to another.
Suzy's thinking: "This won't do
I will not let go of you.
Reassemble me, you fool,
Or you'll go to Reform School!"

6

On the house the sun shines bright
But in the sky there hangs night
And so Good Morning and Good Night

7

Peter and Pussy (begging your pardon)
Do nasty things in kindergarten;
Look at the pigs!
The other children stand and stare.
Teacher Abby says, "Look there—
Ugh, what pigs!"
Flashes her pointed pen,
Waves it in rage; Abby then
Writes: "Dear parents—dissipated lot—
Look what nasty kids you've got!
Can't you give us something better?"
Debauched parents then reply:
"Dear Abby: We sure try.
Now we marry, now divorce—
Makes all kinds of kids, of course."

[1968]   *William Jay Smith*

Toccata

What I feel
as the years are massed:
my life grows
into the past,

my roots burrow
down and down,
history is
my burden.

My childhood:
fairy and gnome,
there was no TV,
no radio,

horses and donkeys
trotted by the hundred,
on the roads a rare
motor blundered,

followed fast
by the hurry-and-scurry
of a gang of boys
in gawking foray.

The sky was empty,
a meadow of blue
not one plane
streaked through.

Electricity, trains:
bright emanations
of some far-off
toy stations.

My fifty years
sink further:
grandfather,
great-grandfather

I shred off
from hearsay,
piece together
from memory,

Klapka and Perczel
I knew long ago,
calling to each
"My dear fellow!"

since even Rákóczi
or Drugeth can
see me as
an old beggarman.

Such an age it's
appalling to be!
Even Plato might
have looked at me,

except that my odd
body would rate
no come-on like
pretty-boys' fate.

When not even
man was there,
the fern-bush bent
over my lair,

called me granddad,
did that fern.
Never, was when
I was born.

Two good handfuls
of dust I brought,
lightly, from
creation's plot,

a roving nobody,
my name a
mix of Love,
Amor, Maitreya,

I have been here
from the beginning of things
but I die with
the butterfly's wings.

[1969]   *Edwin Morgan*

Aphorisms

Word chases its meaning.

*

Dust hurries; stone takes its time.

*

Am I to take part in my own funeral?

*

You are here with your beautiful distance.

*

The tomb listens.

*

Coffin, naked virgin.

*

If born to your daughter, you are immortal.

*

The motionless approaches all the time.

*

Form is motionless, only its appearance dances.

*

Dangernightly.

*

Vapor thorn.

*

Icecomb.

*

Snowhorse.

*

Windcrystal.

*

Rustling water, sky.

*

They twine into a frameless looking-glass.

*

Here we lie, running around.

*

Your unknown selves.

*

Life is never alone.

*

For the second time the first gets lost.

*

Shadesong.

*

I am two, subject and object;
only death can make me one.

*

More and more lonely gods.

[1969]   *William Jay Smith*

At the End of Life

I have been dozing throughout my entire life.
The sights, as in a dream, have revolved;
I did not do anything, things just happened:
I wrote my thousands of verses half-awake,
in tobacco-smoke, I don't even know how.
From my adolescence until now
feminine government so bundled me in cotton-wool and
dulled me that I was unable to act, to live;
I was napping at noon, and wrote at night,
flew like a bat in the dark,
opened inner eyes instead of outer ones.
If in the meantime wisdom or stupidity,
suffering, anything roused me,
my boiler was too strong, it never exploded;
everything was seething, boiling, pressing inside.
Two world-storms raged, a hundred million
people perished, my mother and father died:
all that was not enough to rouse me from my sleep;
however ashamed I am of it, that is the truth.
I experienced everything projected on a screen,
even when it was I who was being chased
to go and tend the pigs, dig graves, or when
shots whistled around my head,
I was asleep all the while, unresponsive. But now
that age shakes my limbs
and clinks glasses with bones beneath my skin:
I would like at last to wake up and run,
to gulp down missed lusts,
to rejoice, and regretting joy, to hurt,
and to die, crippled by my too-late pleasures,
lost in stench, filth, and shame,
a mad dog on a dungheap.

But, as with everything else, I am also only dreaming this.
If until now I have never awakened, I know
I'll go on snoring until I die. Dying perhaps
will make me face awake
the burden of all that I have neglected. Perhaps
in the silence beyond sleep, I shall awaken.

[1969]   *William Jay Smith*

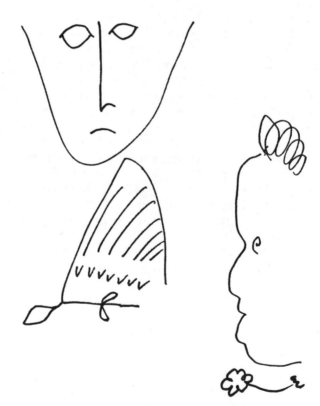

A GIFT TO AUNTIE

from the *Eleventh Symphony*

STAR MUSIC

gigantic current of infinite lines
whirling spin of swirling inner light
inner night gigantic whirling lines

distant blue claws of locked bridge-spans
lines infinite inner night's locked spans
spin of swirling distant blue bridge-spans
gigantic current of infinite lines

enlarging music of living falling stone
bridge-spans claws of whirling lines
enlarging music of infinite locked spans
distant blue inner night spin of falling stone
enlarging music of swirling inner night
its whirling spin gigantic current

huge deadly bird crossing pale shadow
living bridge-spans whirling lines
infinite falling stone distant blue inner night
huge bird's enlarging living claws
bridge-span's whirling spin claws
pale big bird's distant blue music
swirling inner night's gigantic current

your guiding star puts out its nightlamp
enlarging music of locked bridge-spans
living falling stone your guiding star
puts out its nightlamp huge deadly bird
crossing pale shadow whirling infinite
swirling nightlamp of locked falling stone
put out by huge bird living inner blue
whirling spin of deadly falling stone
gigantic current of your guiding star

A CIRCULAR TOUR

In leafy blueness Eden circles, and the
air hides its lightning flashes, here a spring
bubbles up, a column beside it, an oak
tree behind it, in a forest clearing the sky shines naked
without cloud cover; how many birds
flutter their wings, you can't see one there are
so many; how many flowers, clumps of flowers, bloom, all
caressed by sunlight, all entangled in
the single star of a sunlit moment
here and now, the spring nearby; farther on,
the oak tree and the column, Eden circles
leafy blue as our walk advances:
then comes the oak tree, the spring turns away
and the column grows taller, to the rhythm
of slow steps, the place inhabits a tent of light
and the moment's bright star breaks through
the sunlight while our walk winds on:
a white marble column comes into view, farther on
the oak tree and the spring, how many flowers and
birds sparkle, all part of the caress of sunlight,
here many times, steps, as arching
forward, creak on the pebbles before the foaming
spring, the column diminishes, the oak tree
rises, the space around unfolding on all sides;
and time is a star taking shape, here again
the oak tree untouched by any axe; behind, the column
and the spring; what an array of birds in the thick foliage as
the walk winds down, now the hand-sculpted
column is near, farther on, the spring and the oak tree, the walk's
turning is human, lulling you to sleep,
here any time, while the air pulls in
its claws, and Eden circles in leafy blue;
here is the eternal spring at the center; to the right, the
column, to the left, the oak tree, part of the caress of sunlight,
here and foreover, blinds you to sleep, as our walk starts back.

———

ELAN

Glides along midnight, holding up her lamp
in a light loose cloud, cut apart by light,
dances off on surf, russet-velvet clad,
veiled in purple air, seashore cutting in
below the mountain edge which the water bites,
    runs off through the pines, to the clearing comes—
from where do you rise so the wind of the sea
never ripples your cloak, nor your shadow pass
on the ribs of the reef where the breakers break
nor your shadow touch the conical peaks
that align the shore nor the desert space
bear the print of your shape yet the clumsiest hut
is a place of love when you come there; where do
you go to, heavenly one? What do you intend?
What do you plan with our brushwood fire
whose flaming teeth never reach your steps
floating off above the wasps of fire, and the flaming
roses, leaving embers, cinders, cold, flying ash
only sorrow, desire, and black greed—O
naked reality of heaven, to what home do you call me?
    passes to midnight, now into the clouds,
    now beyond the clouds, topped with heaven's bowl,
    now her space uncut, and herself not hid,
    with no sleep her eyes and her heart no lid,
    with her grace unwilled and her heat untold
    with her words unsaid and her name unharmed
unblessed her desire to aid—not until
iron chains no more keep the bull's head down
and rats and snails guard the treasure trove
and children are fed on the blood of pigs
will the great goddess give up being cruel

[1970]   *William Jay Smith*

Customs Clearance

Madam, before we board the crowded bus of desire
where we shall all be happy
let me twist your arms behind your back
and examine your valuables
and take out that refrigerator,
from your handkerchief remove those three corner houses,
the paintings stolen from the museum,
this dead foetus is yours isn't it
and the biggest of those corpses is your husband perhaps
or your highly respected father,
no oh no
madam you misunderstand me I don't want to pay court
                                                      to you

merely a question of duty
thank you

[1970]   *Hugh Maxton*

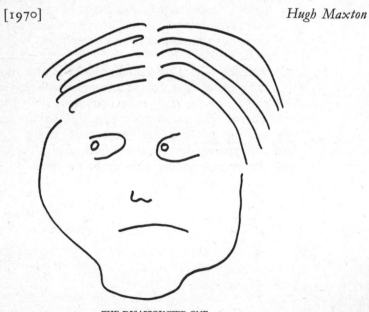

THE DISAPPOINTED ONE

Millennia

A masterpiece is vulnerable,
the wilderness is invulnerable;
reality is unbelievable,
falsehood is believable.

[1980]   *William Jay Smith*

Dice Game

to be lost then found again
my whole life has been that way
it was good to sit beside the sea
to let the waves wash over me

my whole life has been that way
to be lost then found again
to let the waves wash over me
it was good to sit beside the sea

to let the waves wash over me
it was good to sit beside the sea
to be lost then found again
my whole life has been that way

it was good to sit beside the sea
to let the waves wash over me
my whole life has been that way
to be lost then found again

[1980]   *William Jay Smith*

Eternity

The earth, where the living grow,
the all-devouring grave,
the plain, the mountain, the sea, the river:
seems to be eternal and is transient.

Space and firmament,
the many revolving celestial relations,
the billion flame-spheres:
seem to be eternal and are transient.

What is buried by oblivion,
a lizard's creep, a wing's flutter,
a tremor that spins away:
seems to be transient and is eternal.

Because what occurred once
will not be changed by any order,
either by God or by devil:
it seems to be transient and is eternal.

[1980]   *William Jay Smith*

Bolero

We all go away, from under the swaying trees we all go away,
under the humid sky we all set out across the wasteland
to a place beneath the dry sky, all of us who have come together,
some of us still looking back, the moon's beam moves in our
footprint,
in the end we all go away, the sunlight too lags behind
and we are walking behind the stars on the hoops of the sky,
above the spires, some still look back and desire to see
a fallen apple in the garden, or perhaps a cradle
next to the door, under a red awning, but it is late, let us go,
as the bells toll we all amble
always in a different way behind the stars, on the round wall
of the plain,
all who have in the end come together, we all go away.

[1980]   *William Jay Smith*

Supplication

Invisible circular bands on which celestial fires revolve,
underneath you like an ant I carry a single morsel

and I collapse under the weight of my dowry:
I wish I had a ray of your power, circular-orbited stars.

O the weight of the unknown burden! From eternity you have
known,
from eternity to eternity you are not ashamed to bear it,

thus you turn the whole world around, courageously, gracefully
but I myself am a single sliver of your ore: what am I capable of?

[1980]   *William Jay Smith*

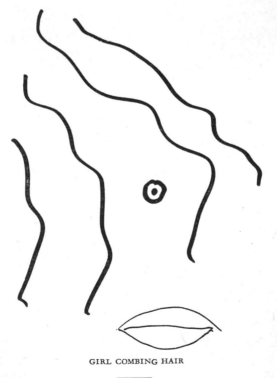

GIRL COMBING HAIR

Prayer

I salute you with the roar of rivers,
the cloud-faced mountains, the mountain-formed clouds,
the gong-shaped stars,
I salute you with the rainbow, with all the fires of night,
and finally with the sun's amazing radiance:
they are all yours! in each you are present,
even if you slumber and even when unexpectedly you come
                                           down to us
and to the host of creations again and again throw light upon
the stiff cold milestones and on your round shields lying about
                                           in the living field,
in the eternal secret of their simplicity, in the mystery of their
                                           openness,
which, because of their constant presence,
we always so easily forget.

[1980]   *William Jay Smith*

El Greco's Parable of Genius

I walk by myself
at night, in the dark.
Someone lights a candle
in the distance.

In his country house
he burns the wick
that hardly illuminates
the depth of his room.

In the twilight moves
the master of the candle,
its flickering flame
is little more than nothing.

But to the wanderer
it is a guiding signal,
to be seen miles away
in the blind night.

Its flicker marks
the direction of my village
like a huge bonfire
across the night.

[1980]   *William Jay Smith*

Space

1

We can hear now,
through all the noise,
the silence of the stars.
Beyond the window
boundless space.
Infinity's
remotest corner
is guarded by a pine tree,
swaying,
and farther down
by a few blades of grass,
by mute, massive earth.

2

A gnarled shadow
lurks at the foot of the fence
when night settles down
it unfolds
slowly floods over everything
like the root of the world,
its black truth.

3

By emptiness
the valley is permeated.
By emptiness
mountains are surrounded.
With emptiness
our rooms are padded
within and without;
with emptiness
we have lived
from primeval times
and do not even notice it.

[1980]   *William Jay Smith*

The Dark Horsemen

At night a rumbling
    breaks my rest:
armored horsemen
    gallop past;
around them yellow
    torches flare
against the houses
    standing there.

Where am I? When?
    I do not know
if I live here now
    or lived there then.
Torches below;
    stars overhead.
I slowly wake
    to find I'm dead.

[1980]   *William Jay Smith*

L'heure bleue

Night so near
lights its first node.
Giantess blue hair
spins along the road.

Hair casts all in blue,
the walls, the doorway,
the lamp-lit window,
a passer-by.

Shadow turns azure,
is slowly blackening,
as the ghost of blue
rivets the evening.

[1980]   *Hugh Maxton*

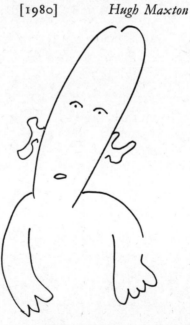

SPORTS FAN

Metronome

A tap out of order and dripping
at night in a dark room
is like footsteps of some swift wanderer.
Clip-clop clip-clop—so it hurries
into black empty silence.
The sound impresses red points
inside the cheeks of the wall;
is near and vast like space.
The chair and table listen
though they are deaf and dumb.
A tap out of order and dripping
at night in a dark room
roams covert regions
—sunless, moonless—
roams the level highway of death
with its foresttracks,
roams inky solitude's
valleys and escarpments.
Clip-clop clip-clop—so it advances
and stays just as it was in the same place.

[1980]   *Hugh Maxton*

The Alchemist

Roaming white speculative planes
and dulled to love's transaction
he discounts his real passion
for those limits where rough life reigns.

He smiles on all invention
computing its weight as none,
accepts the dear objection
his own dense formulae own.

Icepacked in interstellar fury,
yet pure as the golden cygnet
drossed and dressed in mercury,

he roams to infinity, yet
back with fevered Iseult he
is Tristan seeking the first clue.

[1980]   *Hugh Maxton*

Renaissance

It was the era of masks
and the bird saluting the well.

Eyes opening to knowledge
cobbled the dark alleys.

Solid ruins stepped from the past
and mixed with present dilapidation.

Wombshaped, pluckable instruments
contended with huge baggy keyboards.

Born in pain
sincerity
was promptly dying.

Anyone who thought to speak
was already overheard.

The city was full of expectation;
the country with countless flowers,
and unsuspected silky tunes
flew, like a mist of cuckoos, far off.

[1980]   *Hugh Maxton*

Posterity

Past ages strike hollowly in the heart;
echo here, bewail their folly more than loss,
bewail haste and conflict, victory even more so;
while we struggled to get here, to the very edge,
they had taken a toll and it was vanity.
Now man sits on his ruins in rented oblivion.
He retires to his little life, hammers, reaps,
prepares papers as well he might, seldom
looks at the sky where the steeds
of his old aspiration ironically canter,
escapees, beasts of his disintegrating weapons.

[1980]   *Hugh Maxton*

A COMPLICATED COUPLE

Song: Boundless Space

When I was no one yet,
light, clear light,
in the winding brooks
I often slept.

As I almost became someone,
a great force rolled me,
stone, rough stone,
ice-veined, down the slope.

And, finally, I have brightened
to live, flame, naked flame,
in rounded, boundless space,
showing our real country.

[1980]   *William Jay Smith*

AFTERWORD
The Challenge of Weöres

For worthwhile poetic translation, it has always seemed to me, two things are required: a devotedness towards the task in hand, and a certain empathy between the translator and his chosen poet. The professional skill and agility of the first requirement will take the translator so far, but it is only when he can project himself confidently and happily into the mind of the target poet that his work gains the lift and fluency we all want to see. The work of Sándor Weöres is often difficult; it is characterized by unusual variety of form, content, and 'voice'; and it must therefore offer the most acute of challenges to a would-be translator. By a lucky chance, I found that my own approach to poetry coincided at several points with that of Weöres: I have always enjoyed the use of many different voices and personas, I like variety of verse technique from the most free and exploratory to the most strict and metrical, and I relish giving immediacy to distant or mythical events in place and time. Although in other respects there are important differences between us, I felt that I had a certain *entrée* into Weöres's poetry. This did not mean it would be plain sailing! I had to test myself against the very formidable talent which produced on the one hand the intricately rhyming but metrically irregular ten-line stanzas of "The Lost Parasol" and on the other hand the blocked-out non-syntactical visual patterning (allied to concrete poetry) of "Wallpaper and Shadows". Could the same poet possibly have written these two poems? Yes! But I could only show this by showing that I myself, as poet-translator, took joy in both poems, however far apart they might seem. Wherever possible, I tried to deal with the virtuosic technical effects for which this author is famed, though I realized that this must not be at the expense of the deep meditative concern with man's fate—the casting of aesthetic bread over enormous waters of history and wonder and possibility—that was equally a part of Weöres. The bitingly humorous, obsessional *majom*-compounds of "Monkeyland" (*Majom-ország*), the international allusions and ironic collage/camouflage of the unpunctuated (but rhyming!) "Le Journal", the moving, pared-down, short-line stanzas of "For my Mother", the smooth shimmering Horatian verse of "To the Moon"—in each case the problem is that one is not steadily and clearly deepening one's acquaintance with a poet's 'style' but having to adjust to the *ad hoc* precision of a series of poetic solutions. Although eventually one may feel there is such a thing as 'a Weöres poem', this is necessarily qualified by the element of suprise, of exploration and discovery, which he guards as the ultimate prerogative of a man writing for an unknown future.

The challenge he offers is the challenge of a great poet; he keeps his translator stretched, even in his light and playful poems; the reward of any success is that this uniquely rich and distinctive poetry should become more familiar in the English-speaking world.

EDWIN MORGAN

NOTES ON THE TRANSLATORS

ALAN DIXON was born in 1936, near Liverpool. He has been a regular translator of poetry for *The New Hungarian Quarterly* for many years and has contributed to several volumes of Hungarian poetry in translation. His first collection of poems was published by the Fortune Press in 1964. Three others have come from Poet & Printer, the most recent being *The Immaculate Magpies* (1982) which is decorated with his own woodcuts.

DANIEL HOFFMAN was among the principal translators in Miklós Vajda's anthology *Modern Hungarian Poetry* (1977). In 1980 he received the Hungarian P.E.N.'s Memorial Medal. He is the author of several books including *Brotherly Love* and *Able Was I Ere I Saw Elba,* and served as the 1973–74 Consultant in Poetry to the Library of Congress. He is Poet in Residence and the Schelling Professor of English at the University of Pennsylvania.

HUGH MAXTON, born in Dublin in 1947, has published several collections of poetry, including *At the Protestant Museum* (1986) which he wrote in Budapest during the winter of 1983. He began translating Hungarian poetry in 1982 with Mária Kőrösy of the Hungarian P.E.N. Club, and has completed a selection of Ágnes Nemes Nagy's poems for co-publication by Corvina, Budapest and Dedalus Press, Dublin.

EDWIN MORGAN was born in Glasgow in 1920. He was Titular Professor of English at Glasgow University until 1980. He has published many collections of poetry and translations: his *Selected Poems* appeared in 1985, and his selected translations, *Rites of Passage,* in 1976. His earliest Weöres translations appeared in the Penguin Modern European Poets *Selected Poems* of Weöres and Juhász in 1970. He was awarded the Hungarian P.E.N. Memorial Medal in 1972, and a Soros Translation Award in 1985.

WILLIAM JAY SMITH, poet, critic, anthologist and translator, has been translating modern Hungarian poetry since, as Poetry Consultant to the Library of Congress, he first visited Budapest in 1970. He is one of the founders of the Translation Center at Columbia University and an editor of *Translation,* the journal published by the Center. He is the author of *Army Brat,* a memoir, and *The Traveler's Tree : New and Selected Poems,* both published in 1980. Recent books include his translation of Jules Laforgue's *Moral Tales* (1985) and the anthology, co-edited with Dana Gioia, *Poems from Italy.*

GEORGE SZIRTES was born in Budapest in 1948. He was brought up in England, studied Fine Art in Leeds and London, and began exhibiting paintings and publishing poems at roughly the same time. He lives in Hitchin where he works as an art teacher. He has published four collections of poetry: his first, *The Slant Door,* was joint recipient of the Geoffrey Faber Memorial Prize in 1980. Many of the poems in *The Photographer in Winter* (1986) were prompted by his first return journey to Hungary in 1984. He has translated the nineteenth-century epic drama by Imre Madách, *The Tragedy of Man,* for Corvina.

HUNGARIAN TITLES

Printed in Hungary, 1988
Kossuth Printing House, Budapest